GMDSS
UNDERSTANDING THE GLOBAL MARITIME DISTRESS AND SAFETY SYSTEM

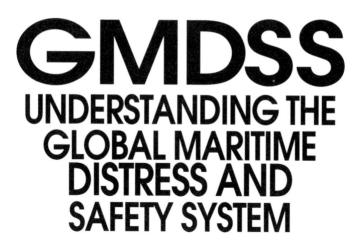

GMDSS
UNDERSTANDING THE GLOBAL MARITIME DISTRESS AND SAFETY SYSTEM

The New Marine Radio Communications System

John Campbell

WATERLINE

First published in the UK in 1998
by Waterline Books, an imprint of Airlife Publishing Ltd

British Library Cataloguing-in-Publication Data
A catalogue record for this book
is available from the British Library

ISBN 1 84037 010 6

Typeset by Servis Filmsetting Ltd, Manchester
Printed in England by MPG Books Limited, Bodmin, Cornwall.

Waterline Books
an imprint of Airlife Publishing Ltd
101 Longden Road, Shrewsbury, SY3 9EB, England

Acknowledgements

Thanks to all those who have supplied information and have helped put this book together: Ed Brady at the Spectrum Management Division of the US Coast Guard, Mike Donner at NIMA, Roger Horner at E^3 Systems in Mallorca, Robin George at ICS Electronics Ltd., Jim Rogers from Friday Harbor, Peter Coles at Waterline, and last, but by no means least, Lana, for helping to organise and correct the typescript.

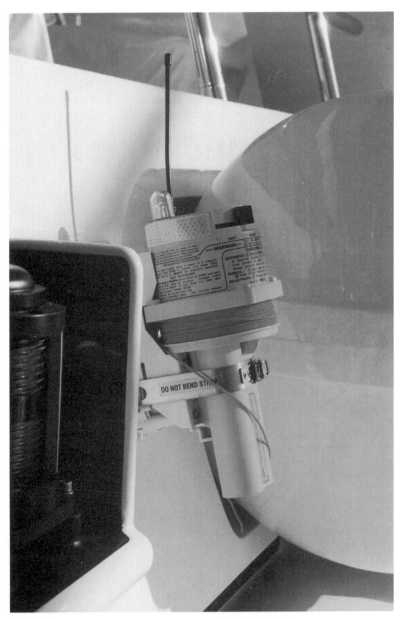

A 406 MHz EPIRB in float-free mount. Test procedure is described on the label.

Contents

Introduction

The **G**lobal **M**aritime **D**istress and **S**afety **S**ystem (GMDSS) is changing the way we communicate at sea. All vessels over 300 tons, and all vessels carrying passengers, are obliged to comply with the regulations. These vessels must carry one, or in some cases two operators who hold a GMDSS certificate. Other vessels do not need to comply with all the GMDSS rules, but they will have to operate within the system if they wish to communicate with GMDSS vessels, if they want to communicate to shore through Coast Stations, or need to raise the alarm in case of distress.

This book has been written not only to help those who are studying for their GMDSS General Operator Certificate, but also for people sailing on board vessels which do not have to comply with the GMDSS regulations, to help them understand the GMDSS, and to show them how they can operate within the system.

Inmarsat M antenna mounted on the spreaders of a sailing yacht.

CHAPTER 1

GMDSS – An Overview of the System

To enter the world of GMDSS is to enter a world of initials, acronyms and abbreviations. The very fact that the **G**lobal **M**aritime **D**istress and **S**afety **S**ystem is known by its initials should serve as a warning. In fact the British GMDSS operator's certificate gets to page 7 before it uses the title in full.

It is virtually impossible to discuss the GMDSS without resorting to the various initials, acronyms and abbreviations, and an appendix is included in the back of this book explaining (all or most of) them. Listed together, they look pretty daunting, but I strongly suggest that you do *not* sit down and try to learn them at the beginning. As we come across each new set of initials or acronym, the full 'translation' will be written out at least once, with the relative initial letters in bold type, and if we go far without using it, I will try and remember to use the 'translation' again. If all else fails, then there is the appendix!

There will be some acronyms that are already familiar, such as EPIRB for the **E**mergency **P**osition **I**ndicating **R**adio **B**eacon. Hopefully there will be some more familiar friends that appear, and by the end of the book, at least the more important ones will have been learnt by use and repetition.

Let's start by looking at who has to comply with the GMDSS regulations. Since 1 February 1995, all new vessels over 300 gross registered tons (and after 1 February 1999, all vessels over 300 tons, and all passenger vessels), must comply with the GMDSS regulations. This includes all commercial vessels, and all yachts over 300 tons, even if privately operated, and all vessels deemed to be passenger vessels.

Smaller vessels, not classed as passenger vessels, do not have to comply, but it is probably in their interest to be able to operate within the GMDSS, because when the system is fully operational, there will be few people

11

listening to the old emergency calling frequencies. If a vessel is seeking help, or indeed, trying to call almost anybody else, it will be much easier to do so within the GMDSS than by using the old methods.

What is the Global Maritime Distress and Safety Service?

It is an attempt by the International Maritime Organisation, one of the world bodies which regulates international shipping, to standardise and improve the methods of radio communication at sea, so that hopefully everybody is able to communicate with everybody else. As we shall see, there is a strong emphasis on safety, as well as routine calling.

When GMDSS was proposed, it was given nine functions.

1. Transmission of ship-to-shore distress alerts by at least two separate and independent means, each using a different radio-communication service.
2. Reception of shore-to-ship distress relay alerts – such as advising vessels that there is a distress situation in their vicinity.
3. Transmission and reception of ship-to-ship distress alerts.
4. Transmission and reception of search and rescue co-ordination communications.
5. Transmission and reception of on-scene distress communications ('on-scene' meaning at the site of a search or rescue).
6. Transmission and reception of signals for locating a vessel in distress.
7. Transmission and reception of maritime safety information.
8. Transmission and reception of general radio-communications to and from shore-based radio systems or networks.
9. Transmission and reception of bridge-to-bridge communications.

At first glance, one might wonder what all the fuss is about. We could do all or most of these things before. Is this so different from what we have been using so far? The short answer is yes, it is different. The reason it is so different is because of the Digital Selective Calling technology, which now controls much of the radio equipment. The DSC control unit is the heart and soul, or perhaps a better analogy would be to call it the mind, of the GMDSS.

Introduction to Digital Selective Calling

DSC is a method of sending alerts, in the form of short messages, which can be specifically addressed to other stations. Such alert messages can be sent to 'all stations', which means that they will be received by everybody within range, or they can be limited to vessels in a specific area, a particular group of vessels, or even to an individual vessel or Coast Station. Stations which are not included in the address will not receive anything.

A DSC control unit receives an alert, sounds an alarm, and displays a short message, so in effect it acts rather like a personal pager. The alert indicates that somebody is trying to reach the vessel, and on what frequency, and in which mode the traffic will be transmitted. The traffic intended for the vessel could be by voice or telex. The DSC alert will also indicate whether the traffic is going to be a distress, urgency, safety or a routine call for traffic. In the case of a distress alert, the position of the distressed vessel is normally included. The alert also gives the identity of the transmitting station, using the **M**aritime **M**obile **S**ervice **I**dentity number. This MMSI number has nine digits – Coast Stations always start with 00, and the next three digits indicate the country – 232 for the UK. For 'maritime mobile' stations, the first three digits indicate the country – e.g. 232 indicates a UK licensed vessel.

The DSC control unit works in a similar manner when you wish to send a message. It will transmit an alert on a special radio frequency – on **V**ery **H**igh **F**requency (VHF), **M**edium **F**requency (MF) or one of the **H**igh **F**requency (HF) bands, according to where you are trying to send the message, or it will even transmit the alert on several bands in the case of a distress alert. It can address the alert to 'all stations' in the case of a distress message, to vessels in a particular area for an urgency or safety call, to a group of vessels, such as the competitors in a race, or to an individual vessel or Coast Station.

The DSC alert that you send consists of your identity as your MMSI number, and the nature of the call, i.e. distress, urgency, safety or routine. The DSC control unit will automatically include your position if it is linked to a **G**lobal **P**ositioning **S**ystem (GPS) receiver, or it will give you the opportunity to enter it manually. It will indicate where and how you intend to send the traffic to the station receiving the alert. In the case of a distress message, it can also include some basic information, which can be entered at the touch of a button. It can indicate whether you are, for example, sinking, aground, abandoning ship, on fire, or subject to a pirate attack. If time is really short, and you don't have time to press the extra buttons, it can send an 'undesignated' distress call which, as a minimum, advises anybody within range that you are in trouble.

We will look at this in more detail when we examine the operation of the DSC control unit. It is sufficient at this stage that we understand that the DSC control unit is effectively a two-way paging device, which alerts the receiving station that a particular type of traffic is waiting to be sent to it.

Distress, Urgency, Safety and Routine Calls Defined

We should perhaps just take a moment to remind ourselves of the differences between distress, urgency, safety and routine traffic.

Distress

A distress call signifies that a vessel or person is in grave *and* imminent danger. Under GMDSS rules, a man overboard is a distress situation. Under the old rules it was not, it was only deemed to warrant an urgency call. So just to re-iterate, before sending a distress call, a vessel or person must be in danger, it must be grave and it must be imminent. So running out of fuel does not warrant a distress call, unless the vessel is going to be swept ashore imminently.

A distress message is preceded by the word Mayday on voice, or SOS on telex. SOS was the old Morse code distress signal, but, perhaps sadly, under the GMDSS Morse code has effectively ceased to exist in maritime communications.

A distress call is the only traffic that may be broadcast – that is, transmitted to the world at large. All other traffic must be addressed to somebody, even if it is to 'all stations.'

Urgency

An urgency call is for when help is needed, but the risk to the vessel or person, although serious, is not grave *and* imminent. A situation as outlined above, where a vessel is likely to be swept ashore, (certainly a grave danger,) in a couple of hours (which could hardly be said to be imminent), does not warrant a distress call, but probably does justify sending an urgency call. Similarly, a medical emergency, perhaps when a patient needs evacuation to save his life, could justify an urgency call, but a call seeking medical advice would not.

An urgency call is preceded by the words Pan Pan. Since it is not a distress call, it cannot be broadcast, it must be addressed to somebody, even if it is to 'all stations'.

Safety

A safety call is for reporting severe weather warnings and dangers to navigation, such as reporting missing navigational marks, or advising vessels of the movements of a large ship. Again, such a call must be addressed to somebody, very often to 'all ships' in these cases. A safety call is preceded by the word *Securité*.

Routine

All other types of call are classed as routine. As with all calls, except a Mayday, routine calls must be addressed to somebody. For most routine calls, this is another vessel, or a Coast Station.

Later on we will look at the procedure for each type of call in detail.

GMDSS Areas and Equipment Required for Each Area

As far as the GMDSS is concerned, the world is divided into four areas.

- **A1** Any area within Very High Frequency radio range of a Coast Station equipped with DSC. As we shall see when we come to look at radio propagation, the average range of VHF communication is about 20 to 30 miles, to or from a Coast Station, so Area A1 is generally a coastal strip, about 20 miles wide.
- **A2** Any area, (excluding area A1) within Medium Frequency radio range of an MF Coast Station equipped with DSC. The reliable range for MF signals is about a hundred miles, so area A2 is a strip about 70 miles wide, around most coastlines, outside of the A1 area.
- **A3** This is the area (excluding areas A1 and A2) within range of the Inmarsat geostationary communication satellites. This area is effectively from about 70° north to 70° south.
- **A4** This is the area not included in any of the above. A4 only covers the very high latitudes, beyond about 70° north or south.

Most national radio administrations publish charts of their local waters, indicating A1 and A2 areas.

There are certain safety items which must be carried by all vessels, and other equipment which must be carried for communication in the various areas. At this point we will take a look at what equipment should be carried, and then later, we will go through each item in turn, looking at the operation and maintenance of it.

Vessels which must comply with the GMDSS regulations have to carry all of the following equipment. Vessels which are not obliged to comply with GMDSS can pick and chose what they want to carry, but they would be well advised to carry all or most of the compulsory equipment wherever possible.

- **Navtex Receiver** – for reception of Marine Safety Information, such as weather forecasts or navigational warnings.
- **EPIRB** – for distress alerting. In area A1 this can be a VHF EPIRB, but for operations in areas A2 to A4, it must operate on the Cospas/Sarsat satellite frequency of 406 MHz, or through the Inmarsat E service.
- **Search and Rescue Transponder** – All vessels are supposed to carry a SART (two for vessels over 500 tons), to assist rescue vessels to locate survival craft by radar.
- **Handheld VHF radios** – there should be two waterproof handheld VHF radios (three for vessels over 500 tons), for use in survival craft.

Additional Requirements

- **Area A1** – Vessels operating in area A1 must additionally carry a VHF transceiver which is capable of operation on DSC on channel 70, voice operation on channels 16, 13, 6 and at least some of the Public Correspondence channels.

15

- **Area A2** – For operating in area A2, vessels must carry the equipment for A1, and additionally must carry a Medium Frequency transceiver, capable of operation on 2187.5 kHz on DSC, voice on 2182 kHz and voice or telex on public correspondence channels.
- **Area A3** – Vessels operating in Area A3 have a choice. All the A1 and A2 equipment must be fitted, then there is a choice of having either:

  1. Inmarsat satellite equipment, capable of reception of Marine Safety Information, distress alerting, regional alert watch-keeping and public correspondence by voice or telex.

  or

  2. High Frequency transceiver (can be combined with the MF transceiver), capable of DSC operation on the 4, 6, 8, 12 and 16 MHz DSC frequencies, and communications by voice or telex on the appropriate safety frequencies on each band.
- **Area A4** – has the same equipment list as the HF option for A3.

As we take a look at all the equipment in turn, we will see how, with the items listed, all the criteria for the GMDSS can be met. Before we start going through the equipment, we should go back to first principals, and take a very basic look at radio propagation.

CHAPTER 2

Radio Propagation

How the radio signals get from here to there

When discussing radio propagation, it is all too easy to turn the whole thing into a black art, and mystify everybody. However, it makes life much easier if we have a broad understanding of how a radio works, and why some frequencies behave differently to others. Such knowledge will help us to choose on which band to operate, depending on the time of day, and the location of the station with which we are trying to communicate.

So what is a radio wave? It is a form of electromagnetic radiation. (Don't give up yet, it is not as bad as it sounds!) To put it another way, it is a stream of energy, which is part electrical and part magnetic. The two components of the wave are at right angles to each other, but they are always in phase. That is, the peaks of each component of the wave leave the antenna at the same time.

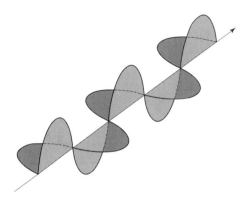

Fig 2.1 Electromagnetic wave

A radio wave travels at the speed of light. In a vacuum, the speed of light is 186,282.4 miles per second. In metric terms this is 299,792,500 metres per second, which, for our purposes, can safely be rounded up to 300,000,000 metres/second. To make these big numbers more manageable, we can express three hundred million as $3x10^8$, which just means 3 with 8 zeros after it.

As we shall see in a moment, it is actually even more convenient for our purposes to write the figure as $300x10^6$ metres per second, which is the same as 300 with 6 zeros after it, or 300 million.

A radio wave can be compared to waves moving across the sea. The wavelength is the distance from the peak of one wave to the peak of the next, or indeed from the bottom of one trough to the bottom of the next. As far as radio waves are concerned, we always measure this distance in metres.

Staying with the sea analogy, if we were to stand on the end of a pier watching a series of waves rolling past us, we could count the number of waves which pass in a minute. This would be the number of cycles per minute, and it is called the frequency of the wave. Because radio waves travel much faster than waves in water, we measure the frequency as cycles per second, or even thousands or millions and sometimes billions of cycles per second.

When we are talking about radio frequencies, we use the term hertz. One Hertz is simply one cycle per second. The term was coined to honour the German physicist Heinrich Hertz who was the first to transmit and receive radio waves in a series of experiments from 1885 to 1889.

Radio frequencies can be very large numbers, and to try to keep them manageable, the metric system of numbering them has been adopted.

> 1,000 Hertz=1 kilohertz (1 kHz)
> 1,000,000 Hertz=1 megahertz (1 MHz) or 1,000 kHz
> 1,000,000,000 Hertz=1 gigahertz (1 GHz, or sometimes 1 gig), which is 1,000 MHz.

For some reason, the abbreviation for kiloHertz is written as kHz, with a small k, yet that for megaHertz is MHz, with a capital M, and gigaHertz is GHz with a capital G. I have no idea why this is so, but I will endeavour to follow the convention.

Radio signals are grouped into bands, according to their frequency. Within each band, specific frequencies are allocated by the International Telecommunications Union (ITU) for particular purposes, so that different users do not all try and transmit on the same frequency, and so interfere with each other. The various bands are broadly defined as:

Very Low Frequency.	3 kHz to 30 kHz	Used mainly for radio navigation aids such as

		Omega, and over-the-horizon military radar.
Low Frequency	30 kHz to 300 kHz	So-called long wave commercial broadcasts. Radio Direction Finding (RDF) beacons, Decca, and Loran navigation systems.
Medium Frequency	300 kHz to 3 MHz	Band for medium wave AM commercial broadcasts, and MF marine communications, including Navtex.
High Frequency	3 MHz to 30 MHz	Short-wave commercial broadcasts and HF marine communications.
Very High Frequency	30 MHz to 300 MHz	Marine VHF communications. Some EPIRBs also use this band.
Ultra High Frequency	300 MHz to 3 GHz	Satellite communications, most EPIRBs, and some radars.
Super High Frequency links.	above 3 GHz	Radar and microwave.

Since all radio waves travel at a constant speed (or near enough for our purposes), it is perhaps, reasonably obvious that if the frequency rises, that is, if more waves pass us per second, then the peaks of the waves must be closer together, or in other words, the wavelength must be shorter. So we can say that:

The wavelength of a signal in metres $=\dfrac{\text{velocity of propagation (metres per sec.)}}{\text{frequency (Hertz)}}$

The symbol for wavelength is λ, and frequency is normally written as f.

Our little formula can be written as: $\lambda=\dfrac{300,000,000}{\text{f Hertz}}$ metres per second

If we take a frequency of 2 MHz, i.e. 2,000,000 Hertz, which we can write as 2×10^6 Hertz, we can calculate the wavelength as:

$$\lambda=\frac{300\text{x}10^6 \text{ (metres per second)}}{2\text{x}10^6 \text{ (cycles per second)}}$$

19

Dividing units of metres per second by units of 'per second' gives us metres, so:

$$\lambda = \frac{300}{2} \text{ metres} = 150 \text{ metres}$$

Therefore, a radio signal having a frequency of 2 MHz has a wavelength of 150 metres.

Now it is probably apparent why we chose to write the velocity of the radio wave as $300 = 10^6$ metres per second. It makes the mathematics much easier.

Conversely, the frequency $f = \dfrac{\text{velocity of propagation (metres per second)}}{\text{wavelength } \lambda \quad \text{(metres)}}$

So for a wavelength of, say, 75 metres we can write:

$$f = \frac{300 \times 10^6}{75} \frac{(\text{ metres per second})}{(\text{metres})}$$

Dividing metres per second by metres we get units of 'per second'

$$f = 4 \times 10^6 \text{ Hertz (cycles per second)}$$
$$= 4 \text{ MHz}$$

Therefore, a radio signal having a wavelength of 75 metres has a frequency of 4 MHz.

Using this very simple formula, if we know the frequency of a radio wave we can calculate the wavelength, and *vice versa*. Shortly we will see why this is important.

Radio waves not only travel at the same speed as light, but share several other properties with light.

- Both travel in a straight line in free space.
- Both can be reflected, as light is reflected by a mirror.
- Both can be refracted, or bent, as a stick in water appears to be bent where it passes through the surface of the water.
- Both can be absorbed. Light is absorbed when it falls on a matt black surface, which is why it looks black – all the light has been absorbed.

These four factors determine how a particular radio wave will be propagated. Radio waves of different frequencies behave in different ways – some are more able to be refracted or bent, while others are more likely to be absorbed.

Propagation of Medium and High Frequency Signals

The atmosphere which surrounds the earth is composed of many different layers. The part of the atmosphere which affects the propagation of radio waves is the ionosphere. This is a region which extends from about 80 to some 400 kilometres above the surface of the earth. (Remember, kilo=1,000, so 80 kilometres is 80,000 metres).

The ionosphere is continuously changing. It is affected by the ultraviolet radiation from the sun, which acts on the various molecules of gas that make up the atmosphere. The radiation causes these molecules to break apart, releasing free ions and electrons, and it is these particles which affect the radio waves, absorbing them, refracting them and reflecting them. If it was not for the ionosphere, then all radio communication would be limited to 'line of sight', or via satellites. Communication satellites act almost like an artificial ionosphere, effectively reflecting radio signals back to earth, to enable radio communication over the horizon.

The ionosphere is not a simple layer, but is in fact composed of many layers, each having different properties and each affecting radio waves in a different way. Just to keep things interesting, the layers of the ionosphere are constantly changing, both in altitude, and in degree of ionisation. As these changes occur, they have a profound effect on the propagation of the radio waves. A radio operator needs to have some idea of the likely state of the ionosphere at any given time, to help in the selection of the most suitable frequency for the transmitted signal, to give it the best chance of reaching the intended destination.

Since it is the sun which ionises the gases to form the various layers, it should not be any great surprise to find that the layers change in height and degree of ionisation not only with the time of day, but with the season too. The effects of the ionisation are strongest at midday in the summer, and weakest at night in winter. There are three layers of the ionosphere which concern us. Rather unimaginatively they have been labelled the D, E and F layers.

D layer

This layer is closest to the earth, at an altitude of about 80 kilometres. The degree of ionisation is directly dependent on the level of radiation from the sun. The layer forms by day and disappears at night, with its effects being strongest in the summer. The D layer tends to absorb any radio waves below about 3 MHz. So, in daylight hours, particularly in the summer, frequencies below 3 MHz are restricted to relatively short distances, mainly using ground wave propagation.

E layer

The E layer remains at a fairly constant altitude of about 100 to 120 kilometres. It exists to some extent all the time, but the degree of ionisation varies with the radiation received from the sun. It becomes most heavily ionised, and hence at its most active around noon. As the intensity of the sunlight decreases, the ions and electrons begin to recombine and the level of ionisation falls rapidly, but a small degree of ionisation persists throughout the 24 hours.

F layer

This layer has the biggest effect on radio transmissions of frequencies between 3 and 30 MHz. During the day, as it becomes ionised, the F layer splits into two layers, F_1 and F_2. These are at an altitude of about 200 and 350 kilometres respectively.

At night, and especially in winter, the ions and electrons slowly recombine to form a single F layer, at an altitude of around 250 kilometres. The level of ionisation falls slowly during the night, to reach a minimum just before dawn.

There are four types of radio wave that we must consider:

- **Space wave** This is a radio wave travelling in free space, in a straight line from one antenna to another. The distance is limited by the curve of the earth and the height of the two antennas. This is the type of wave used in VHF and UHF communications. It is effectively limited to line-of-sight between the two antennas.
- **Ground wave** This wave actually travels along the surface of the earth, so it can go over the horizon, but as it travels, it is absorbed by the earth until it eventually becomes too weak to use.
- **Sky wave** This is the wave which is refracted and reflected back to Earth by the various ionised layers, to permit communication over the horizon. The frequencies that can use the sky wave are between 3 and 30 MHz, and which frequency is selected depends on the degree of ionisation, i.e. time of day and season, and the distance to the receiving station.
- **Escape wave** These are the waves which pass through the ionosphere, either because their frequency is too high for the prevailing ionisation, or the angle at which they meet the ionosphere is too great to permit reflection back to earth. These waves are destined to vanish into space.

As can be seen from fig. 2.2, there is a critical angle where a particular wave gets reflected back to earth, rather than escaping into space. The distance between the transmitter and where this wave reaches the ground is called the skip distance. Part of this distance will be close enough to the transmitter for the ground wave to be received, but in the remainder, there will be no reception, and communication will not be possible on that frequency, in that area. This zone is called the skip zone. The size of the skip zone will vary with the frequency being used, and the degree of ionisation of the various layers. A large part of the skill in operating a radio lies in select-

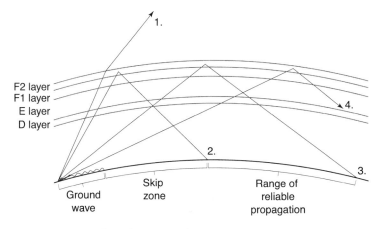

1. Wave not reflected – escapes into space
2. Highest angle of wave that can be reflected back to earth
3. Lowest angle of wave which is reflected and can reach the earth
4. Wave is reflected, but the angle is too low for it to return to the earth

Fig 2.2 HF sky wave propagation

ing the right frequency for the time of day, season and distance over which it is desired to communicate.

A wave which has been reflected back to earth by the ionosphere, can in turn be reflected by the earth, to be returned once again by the ionosphere. Obviously this wave, sometimes called a two-hop wave, has the potential for going further than a single-hop wave. Indeed under good conditions three hops or even more can be made.

While these extra hops can help us when trying to reach large distances, they can sometimes cause problems too. It is entirely possible for a signal to arrive at a receiver by two different paths – by a one-hop and by a two-hop wave.(*See* fig. 2.3)

Since the ionosphere is constantly changing, the paths of these waves are constantly changing too. Sometimes the signals arriving on different paths might be in phase – that is, the peaks of both waves arriving at the same instant, in which case the signal will be extra strong. Alternatively, they may be out of phase – the peaks of one wave arriving with the troughs of the other. In which case the two waves will tend to cancel each other, and so reduce the signal considerably. Such a phenomenon is called fading, and it causes the received signal to vary considerably in strength from one moment to another. This effect can be minimised by using the **A**utomatic **G**ain **C**ontrol on the receiver. When set, the AGC will endeavour to keep the volume constant,

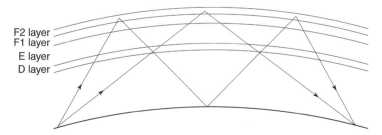

F2 layer
F1 layer
E layer
D layer

Fig 2.3 One-hop and two-hop waves

despite the changing signal strength. We will look at this in more detail when we come to the use and operation of the **High Frequency** radio set.

As we have already noted, the various ionised layers can refract and reflect radio waves. The higher the frequency of a radio wave, then the more intensely must a layer be ionised for it to be able to refract or reflect the wave.

The level of ionisation is also affected by sunspot activity. Sunspots are regions of intense radiation which develop on the surface of the sun. If there are active sunspots, the levels of radiation will increase, causing the degree of ionisation to increase, making it possible to use higher frequencies for longer periods. Sunspot activity is related to an eleven-year cycle – 2003 is a peak year for sunspot activity.

When selecting what frequency to use, it is necessary to know how much daylight or darkness there is between the two stations, to have an approximate idea of the distance, and to be aware of the time of year. As long as we remember that the higher the frequency, the greater the ionisation that is required to reflect the wave, then a basic pattern for frequency choice can be worked out.

22 MHz

This is the highest frequency of the normal marine bands, so we know that it will require the most ionisation. Therefore it will only work in daylight, and it will be more reliable in the summer than in the winter. It will be at its best when it is local noon halfway between the two stations. At other times the ionisation will not be sufficiently strong to reflect the signal, and it will escape through the ionosphere. The band closes as dusk approaches. Because a 22 MHz wave is reflected by the highest layer, the F_2 layer, the skip distance is large. It is always at least 1,000 but often as much as 3,000 miles, so it can only be used for communication over distances greater than this.

During periods of high sunspot activity, the maximum range often exceeds 8,000 miles. This band works better on paths to the north and south rather than to the east or west.

16 MHz

This is still a fairly high frequency, so it too will only work in daylight. It is not quite as critical as 22 MHz, but there will probably not be sufficient ionisation for it to be reflected if it is early morning or late afternoon at either station. The skip distance for 16 MHz is in the order of 800 rising to 2,000 miles, so it can be used for any distances greater than this. Under good conditions of ionisation the maximum range in late afternoon can rise to 6,000 miles or more. As with 22 MHz, 16 MHz will escape through the ionosphere at night and be lost.

12 MHz

This is the highest frequency that can be used both day and night, although its character and properties change with the time of day, and the resulting ionisation. The band starts off weak in the morning, but as noon approaches the maximum range is about 2,000 miles with a skip of about 600 miles.

At night, when the ionisation is less, the wave can still be reflected, but only when it strikes the ionosphere at a very shallow angle. Waves striking at a steeper angle, which would be reflected with no problem in daylight, will escape through the ionosphere at night. This shallower angle results in the wave being returned to earth further from the transmitter than by day, increasing the night skip distance to about 1,000 miles, and the maximum range to about 4,000 miles.

8 MHz

Signals with a frequency in the 8 MHz band will just about always be refracted and reflected, both day and night. Because the signals are so easily reflected, during the day, even those waves striking the ionosphere at very steep angles are reflected back, resulting in a skip distance the same or smaller than the ground wave distance. So often there is no skip zone by day, and communications are normally possible from close to the transmitter to about 1,000 miles, usually without any noticeable dead areas.

By night, when the ionisation is less, the critical angle for reflection becomes shallower, so a skip distance develops of some 300 miles, but the range for useful communications increases to 2,000 miles or more.

6 MHz

This band shares the characteristics of the 8 and the 4 MHz bands. In the summer, when ionisation levels tend to be higher, it will behave much like the 8 MHz band. In the winter, it will be more like the 4 MHz band.

4 MHz

These lower frequencies are very easily refracted and reflected, so now absorption plays a much bigger role. During daylight, the ionosphere, especially the D layer, will tend to absorb the signals. A typical morning maximum range will be about 250 miles. Around the middle of the day, when ionisation is strong, virtually all the signals are absorbed. During the afternoon, the band opens again, allowing communications from 50 to 300 miles. However, at night, as the D layer disappears, the signals can be refracted and reflected by the F layer, and ranges of 2,000 miles or more can be achieved, with a skip zone of about 200 miles. These lower frequencies are much more susceptible to atmospheric noise. This noise level increases with the ionisation level, so it is at its worst by day in the summer, and causes the fewest problems at night in the winter.

2 MHz

These frequencies are readily absorbed by the D layer, so during the day, sky wave propagation is limited to those waves which strike the ionosphere at very steep angles, and so are returned close to the transmitter. This limits the daytime range of the sky wave to about 75 miles.

MF transmissions have a useful ground wave – the lower the frequency, the further the ground wave can travel. Since the signal is absorbed by the earth as it travels along the surface, the more powerful the signal that is transmitted, the further it is able to travel before being lost to absorption. A 2 MHz signal will travel approximately ¾ of a mile for every watt of power used. Because of this phenomenon, most licensing administrations restrict the maximum power output for a marine MF radio to 400 watts.

At night, as soon as the D layer dissipates, then signals at lower angles are reflected by the F layer and sky wave propagation is possible. Reliable communications up to 200 miles are normal, but distances in excess of a thousand miles are not uncommon.

Propagation of Very High Frequencies and Ultra High Frequencies

Signals in the VHF and UHF bands (frequencies over 30 MHz) will not generally be refracted or reflected by the F layer, but occasionally they will be by the E layer. This phenomenon is called Sporadic E. They will also sometimes be refracted by the troposphere – the region beyond the ionosphere. These somewhat unusual conditions account for some of those times when we suddenly hear distant stations being received on the VHF, when they are well beyond the normal range. Some meteorological conditions such as temperature inversions and 'ducting' can also cause unusually distant VHF propagation.

The normal mode of propagation of a VHF or UHF signal is by space wave. There is very little ground wave on these higher frequency bands, and as we have just seen, sky wave is rare, and not reliable.

Although we said that radio waves travel in a straight line in space, they are refracted a little as they pass through the air of the lower atmosphere. This allows a radio space wave to pass over the horizon. The distance to the radio horizon is about a third more than to the visible horizon.

Just as the distance to our visible horizon increases as our vantage point rises, so the distance to the radio horizon increases with the height of the antenna. The distance to the radio horizon is easy to calculate:

The distance in nautical miles $D=2.23\sqrt{\text{height in metres of antenna H}}$.

For an antenna at a height of 25 metres, the distance to the radio horizon will be:

$$D=2.23\sqrt{25} \text{ miles}$$
$$=2.23\text{x}5 \text{ miles}$$
$$=11.15 \text{ miles}$$

To calculate the maximum distance that a radio VHF signal can travel between two antennas of known height, the two distances are added together:

$$D=2.23\sqrt{H}_{\text{transmitter}}+2.23\sqrt{H}_{\text{receiver}}$$

The higher that the VHF antenna can be mounted, the greater the range that it will be possible to transmit or receive signals. This will be particularly noticeable when trying to communicate with a small vessel, or even more so, with a person in a liferaft using a handheld VHF.

Typical ranges, dependent of course on the heights of the antennas concerned are:

Coast Station to/from a large ship with high antenna	–	Range about 60 miles
Coast Station to/from a yacht with masthead antenna	–	Range about 35 miles
Coast Station to/from a handheld VHF radio	–	Range about 15 miles

Yacht-to-yacht with 9 metre antennas	– Range about 13 miles
Yacht with 9 metre high antenna to handheld	– Range about 10 miles
Handheld to handheld	– Range about 5 miles

UHF signals pass through the atmosphere almost without noticing it. They are hardly refracted or absorbed at all by the ionosphere, so the signals continue out in a straight line, which is exactly what is needed for sending and receiving signals between a satellite and a ground station. The satellite in effect is acting like a very high antenna for the station on the ground. Communications between a ground station and a satellite are line-of-sight, so the satellite must be above the horizon when viewed from a mobile station. Normally an elevation of at least 5° is sufficient to ensure good communication. We will look at this further in Chapter 9.

Domes come in all sizes. The biggest is to receive TV signals, the larger one above the bridge windows is Inmarsat A, and the smaller one is to receive satellite weather information.

CHAPTER 3

Antennas

Antenna Types

There are three basic types of antennas which are used for radio communication on board vessels.

1. **Whip Antenna** This type is the rigid, usually white, plastic rod, which is mounted vertically. Whip antennas are just about universally used for Very High Frequency radio transmission and reception. As we saw in the section on propagation, the range of a VHF signal is pretty much dependent on the height of the antenna, so any VHF antenna should be mounted as high as possible. Whip antennas are also sometimes used for Medium Frequency and High Frequency transmission and reception. We will shortly see that lower frequency signals need longer antennas, so whips for MF and for HF will be much larger than for VHF radios.
2. **Wire Antenna** This is exactly what it sounds like – a length of wire, suitably suspended with insulators. If it is suspended vertically, and the signal is fed at one end, then it behaves exactly like a whip. More often though, a wire antenna is suspended horizontally. The signal can be fed from one end of the wire, but sometimes it is fed from the centre, to make what is called a dipole. More on that in a moment.
3. **Dish Antenna** Whips and wire antennas are more or less omnidirectional. That is, they can transmit and receive equally well in all directions. Some satellite communication systems operate at very low power, and they need a very directional antenna to focus the signal into a beam. Such a system uses a dish antenna. The dish itself is not unlike the receiving dish for domestic satellite television, and indeed, if the boat was fixed firmly in one position, virtually the same antenna could be used. However, as we all know, boats move around, all too often quite wildly, so a dish antenna must be fitted with motors and sensors to keep the dish pointed at the satellite while the boat moves. To protect the mechanism and to prevent the wind moving the dish, the antenna is encased in a plastic dome – the ubiquitous mushroom that we see on large yachts and most commercial ships.

For vessels which are required to comply with GMDSS, there are certain rules for antennas.

- A reserve antenna must be fitted (unless specifically exempt) for the main MF/HF transmitter.
- For any suspended wire antenna, a complete spare must be carried, which can be erected if an antenna is lost.
- The halyards for a wire antenna must be wire not rope, so that in the case of fire, the antenna does not come crashing down.
- A weak link, with a breaking strain of ⅙ of that of the antenna itself, must be fitted, together with a safety loop to restrain the antenna if the weak link breaks.
- Compulsory ships are required to carry complete spare units for any whip antennas that are fitted.

Determining Antenna Length

Most antennas will operate most efficiently if they are a half-wavelength long. A half-wavelength can be written as $\lambda/2$. Since we know how to calculate the wavelength for a given frequency, it is easy to work out what the optimum length of an antenna should be. Let's try it for a VHF signal of 150 MHz.

$$\lambda = \frac{300 \times 10^6 \text{ metres per second}}{150 \text{ MHz}}$$

$$= \frac{300 \times 10^6 \text{ metres per second}}{150 \times 10^6 \text{ cycles per second}}$$

$$= \frac{300 \text{ metres}}{150}$$

$$= 2 \text{ metres}$$

So half a wavelength would be one metre, and therefore the antenna should be about a metre long.

However, radio waves travel a little slower in anything other than the vacuum of free space. In the average antenna, the speed is about 95% of the speed in a vacuum, so we must multiply the result by 0.95 to be accurate.

So, the arithmetic for the length of a half-wave antenna becomes:

$$\lambda/2 \text{ antenna} = \frac{150 \times 0.95 \times 10^6}{\text{frequency in Hertz}} \text{ metres}$$

Which can be simplified to:

$$= \frac{142}{\text{frequency in MHz}} \text{ metres}$$

For those who are still determined to work in 'old money', the length of the antenna in metres can be converted to feet and inches (a metre is 3.281 feet, or 39.37 inches), or you can rewrite the formula. Since the speed of light is 984 x 10^6 feet per second, the formula becomes:

$$\lambda = \frac{984 \times 106}{\text{frequency in Hertz}} \text{ feet}$$

$$= \frac{984}{\text{frequency in MHz}} \text{ feet}$$

The length of a half wave antenna becomes:

$$\lambda/2 \text{ antenna} = \frac{492 \times 0.95}{\text{frequency in MHz}} \text{ feet}$$

$$= \frac{468}{\text{frequency in MHz}} \text{ feet}$$

Whichever units you choose to work in, it is worth remembering one of the ways to calculate the length of the antenna, because then it is possible to construct an emergency antenna if the real antenna is lost. Most transmitting antennas need a ground or counterpoise to balance the signal against. An exception is the half-wave dipole. This is an antenna which is fed in the centre, and has a quarter-wave length of wire on either side.

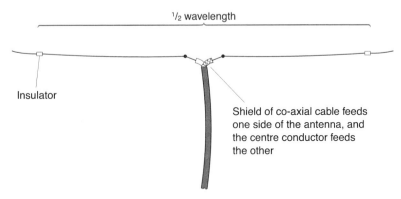

Fig 3.1 Half-wave dipole antenna

Making an Emergency Antenna

With a half-wave dipole, one side of the antenna effectively acts as a ground to the other side, forming a very efficient antenna. For the higher frequencies, a dipole is quite short, and can easily be made for an emergency antenna, especially for the VHF, or the higher HF bands.

A quick and easy dipole for an emergency VHF antenna can be made just by stripping back the insulation on a piece of coaxial cable for half a metre (one quarter wavelength at 150 MHz). The centre conductor can be pulled out from the braided shield, and if both are stretched out at right angles to the cable itself, the result is a dipole antenna, resonant at 150 MHz.

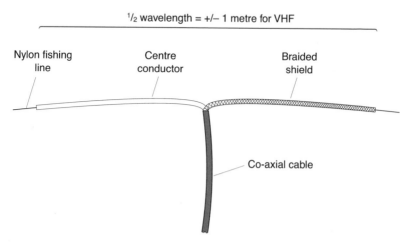

Fig 3.2 Emergency VHF antenna made from coaxial cable and fishing line

Suspend the antenna with a couple of bits of nylon fishing line, or even plastic bags to act as insulators, and you will have a remarkably efficient antenna for the VHF, if the main antenna has been lost or damaged (perhaps after being dismasted). Using the main VHF with its 25 watts of power through such an antenna, will give a much better signal than a little handheld VHF.

A similar emergency antenna could be made for the HF radio, at least for the higher frequencies. A dipole for 16 MHz would have an overall length of less than 9 metres, which would be manageable on most boats. However, for 4 MHz such an antenna would be over 35 metres long – not really feasible except on a large vessel.

Antenna Tuning

Antennas which are not the optimum length can be made to operate on a particular band, or indeed on several bands, by adding various coils and capacitors to the end of the antenna. In this way the radio can be fooled into thinking that the antenna is a perfect length for the frequency on which it is being asked to transmit. A tuner unit is used to do this, and it may require manual operation, usually by means of three rotary switches, or it may be automatic, needing just a push of a button to select the best combination of coils and capacitors for a particular frequency.

Just before we leave antennas, we should take a look at their care and maintenance.

Antenna Maintenance

On wire antennas, the insulators must be kept clean. A build-up of salt or dirt on the insulators will reduce their ability to insulate, and cause a significant loss of signal, so they should be cleaned on a regular basis. Great care must be taken that the transmitter cannot be activated while anybody is near the ends of the antenna. Extremely high voltages are generated at the ends, and they can cause severe injury, or possibly even death.

Any shackles used in the assembly of the antenna should be kept well greased, so that the antenna can be disassembled if there is a problem without having to fight with seized shackles.

Whip antennas too should be kept clean. They are made of glass fibre, which is transparent to the radio frequencies. However, a layer of salt, perhaps mixed with a bit of dirt, will act as a fairly effective shield, stopping the radio waves from reaching the wire antenna inside.

Similarly, the glass fibre dome over a dish antenna must be kept clean for the same reason. The dome must not be painted, except with a special paint, because normal paint is opaque to radio signals. Again, care must be taken not to transmit while anybody is working on or near the dome. The frequencies used for satellite communication are extremely high, and the effect of being close to the dome when the set is transmitting would be akin to putting your head in a microwave cooker – an experience to be avoided.

CHAPTER 4

Basic Radio Theory

It is as well for any radio operator to have a basic idea of how a radio signal is transmitted, but for the purposes of this book, we will have to tread a fine line between oversimplifying the explanation, and getting totally bogged down in the more esoteric theories. Here we go!

We have already seen that a radio signal is an electromagnetic wave. This signal is transmitted at a particular frequency. However, if we were to receive such a signal, all we would be able to hear would be a continuous tone. For us to receive any 'intelligence' from the signal, it must be varied in some way to convey the information. In radio terms, the signal is modulated.

There are several ways in which a signal can be modulated. The earliest way was to simply turn the signal on and off. This could be done to a pattern, and so we got the familiar dots and dashes of Morse code. Such patterns of tone were fine for sending letters or numbers in code, but the sound of voices could not be transmitted in this way with any real degree of success.

This on-and-off tone works surprisingly well when the code is being received by the human ear. Machines such as computers are not quite so good at detecting when a tone is turned on or off, so a more modern version was developed. Rather than switching the tone on and off, it is switched between two frequencies. This is called **F**requency **S**hift **K**eying. FSK is widely used for the transmission of data and telexes, and we will come across it again when we take a look at how telexes work.

Amplitude Modulation

For the sound of a voice to be transmitted, the continuous tone, or carrier wave as it is called, must be varied, or modulated, according to the frequency of the sound waves of the voice. The carrier wave is transmitted at a fixed frequency, which is the **R**adio **F**requency. The ever-changing sound waves from the voice become the **Audio Frequency.** When the RF and the AF signals are combined, this gives us four signals to consider:

- The original RF signal – the carrier wave
- The original AF signal – the voice intelligence
- The upper sideband – the sum of the RF and the AF signals
- The lower sideband – the difference between the RF and the AF signals.

The two sidebands, because they are both functions of the same two initial signals, are mirror images of each other.

To prevent signals taking up too much space on the radio band, the modulation is limited to 3 kHz either side of the carrier frequency. This type of modulation is called **Amplitude Modulation,** and because both sidebands are being transmitted, it is referred to as double sideband. This kind of modulation is the AM modulation of most medium and long-wave commercial broadcasts that you might receive on a domestic radio.

The International Telecommunication Union has given a designation to each type of radio transmission, and they are labelled in the format letter-number-letter. The first letter signifies the type of modulation. There are five letters which classify the signals that concern us:

A **A**mplitude **M**odulation. Double sideband
H **A**mplitude **M**odulation. Single sideband with full carrier
R **A**mplitude **M**odulation. Single sideband with reduced carrier
J **A**mplitude **M**odulation. Single sideband with suppressed carrier
F **F**requency **M**odulation.

The middle number of the designation indicates the type of information carried by the signal. There are three of them which we might use:

1 Digital information without a modulating sub-carrier
2 Digital information with a modulating sub-carrier
3 Analogue information.

The last letter of the designation tells us how the signal is supposed to be received. The letters of interest to us are:

A Telegraphy for aural reception (such as Morse code)
B Telegraphy for automatic reception (such as telex or DSC)
E Telephony – voice signals.

AM double sideband is A3E. (One way to remember **A**3E is to think of the signal as having **A**ll the components i.e. carrier and both sidebands.) The '3' signifies analogue information and the 'E' tells us that it is voice. A3E is the modulation of commercial AM medium wave broadcasts.

If we look at this diagramatically, for an A3E signal being transmitted on

35

2182 KHz (the International Distress Frequency), we can see that for a hundred watts of power, perhaps 50 watts goes into the carrier wave, and 25 watts into each sideband.

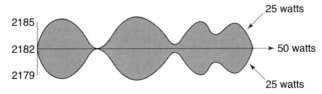

Fig 4.1 AM double sideband signal (A3E)

All the intelligence of this AM double sideband signal is conveyed in each of the sidebands. It was soon realised that if one of the sidebands could be eliminated, then the power that it had been using could go into the other sideband. Single **S**ide**B**and was born.

The earliest SSB transmissions retained the carrier wave, and just one of the sidebands – for marine communication, the upper sideband was selected. With this system the same 50 watts goes into the carrier, but now, 50 watts can go into the sideband, the part of the signal which carries the intelligence, so the effective power of the transmitter is doubled.

Fig 4.2 Single sideband with full carrier (H3E)

Such a signal, with one sideband suppressed, is still **A**mplitude **M**odulated, but it is termed Single Sideband, with full carrier. It is classed as **H**3E. (One way to remember this is to think of it as having the w**H**ole of the carrier wave.)

The next stage was to reduce the power still being 'wasted' by the carrier wave. For the intelligence of the sideband to be converted back to AF, to give the sound of the voice, the carrier wave must be present in the receiver. The first step was to reduce the power of the carrier which was being transmitted, and to have it re-inserted in the receiver. By receiving the reduced carrier, the receiver knew exactly where to re-insert the carrier. If the carrier is reduced to say 10 watts, the sideband can now get 90 watts, almost doubling the power again.

A single sideband signal with reduced carrier is classed as R3E. (**R**3E is **R**educed carrier.) Until recently many SSB radios had a switch to allow them to transmit in R3E. This would help the receiver to insert the carrier in the right place when reception was difficult. Few new transmitters now have this

Fig 4.3 Single sideband with reduced carrier (R3E)

facility, as most modern receivers have no problem re-inserting the carrier in the received signal.

As solid state technology improved the ability of receivers it became possible to suppress the carrier altogether and simply transmit the sideband. This allows all the transmitted power to be used by the sideband. When the signal is received the carrier is re-inserted to generate the **Audio Frequency** in the receiver.

Fig 4.4 Single sideband with suppressed carrier (J3E)

A single sideband signal transmitted with a suppressed carrier is called J3E. (Just the sideband is transmitted). This is the normal mode of transmission on **Medium Frequency** and **High Frequency** for all marine communications by voice.

Frequency Modulation

The other type of modulation which is used for voice communications is **Frequency Modulation**. When the **Audio Frequency** signal is applied to the carrier in an FM transmission, the actual frequency of the carrier is altered. It is increased during one half of the cycle and decreased during the opposite half of the cycle. The change in frequency, called the deviation, is proportional to the amplitude of the modulating signal. It is this deviation which conveys the intelligence of the signal.

FM has some advantages over AM. A much better signal-to-noise ratio is possible, so there is much less interference from static, or atmospheric noise. FM exhibits a slightly strange phenomenon called the 'capture effect'. If there are two AM signals being transmitted on the same frequency, an AM receiver will receive both, and the listener will hear both, one superimposed on the other. However, an FM receiver, receiving two FM signals on the same frequency will 'capture' the strongest one and ignore the other. So it is virtually impossible to hear two FM stations interfering with each other. This is the reason why, when driving in a car with the radio tuned to an FM broadcast station, one station will suddenly vanish, and a new one appear. This is because you have moved farther from the original station, and now the signal coming from the other station becomes the stronger of the two and it is suddenly 'captured' and the other one is ignored.

The capture effect can be of benefit for reducing interference, as it means that the strongest station is the only one being heard. However, it also means that the signal from somebody using a handheld VHF in a liferaft will be completely obliterated by any stations transmitting a stronger signal. Another problem that we have probably all heard is when somebody's VHF radio sticks in the transmit condition. They are only putting out a carrier wave, but if their signal is the strongest then nobody else can be heard on that frequency.

FM is used on the marine VHF bands. The voice signals are classed as F3E. F for Frequency Modulation, 3 for analogue information and E for voice.

FM is not used on the MF or HF bands because it uses quite a lot of bandwidth due to the deviation of the frequency. This means that transmitting frequencies must be further apart than for SSB transmissions. Space is at a premium between 3 and 30 MHz; just 27 MHz covers all the MF and HF bands which are shared with a variety of services. Marine users get just a fraction of a MHz on each band for their use. Space is not such a problem in the higher bands, where there is a bit more room for everybody. The marine portion of the VHF band covers just over 6 MHz on its own.

Phase Modulation

There is one more way of modulating the signal and that is by modulating its phase. It is sufficient for us to be aware of **P**hase **M**odulation and to know that this is often used in the transmission of data and that the identification letter is G.

Simplex and Duplex Operations

When two stations in communication with each other transmit and receive on the same frequency they are said to be operating 'simplex'. The information can only go in one direction at a time, so each station must take it in turn to transmit while the other receives. When we are operating simplex on voice it is normal to say 'Over' at the end of each transmission, to advise the other station that we are listening and they can transmit.

For two stations to be able to hold a conversation, as one would on a normal telephone where either party can talk whenever they want and each can hear the other, even when they are talking themselves, 'duplex' operation must be used. In duplex operation two frequencies must be used. Take the case of a ship making a telephone call through a Coast Station. The ship will transmit on one frequency and listen on a second. The Coast Station will transmit on the second frequency and listen to the one that the ship is transmitting on. In most installations this requires two separate antennas – one for transmitting and one for receiving.

Many marine installations work in a mode called 'semi-duplex'. In this situation the shore party is working duplex – they can still hear while they are talking, but the ship is working simplex – they can only hear when they are not transmitting. Two frequencies are still being used, but the advantage as far as the ship installation is concerned is that only one antenna is needed.

All public correspondence channels through a Coast Station will be on paired frequencies on VHF, MF or HF, regardless of whether it is for voice or telex communications. The appropriate list of radio signals will indicate the frequencies to be used. For the VHF it will invariably give the channel number rather than frequencies. For the MF and HF it may give an ITU channel number, or it may give the transmit and receive frequencies.

All VHF radios are marked with the channel number rather than the frequency, and most modern MF/HF radios will accept an ITU channel number. However, if you have to enter the transmit and receive frequencies manually, it is vital to get them the right way round. The list of radio signals give the transmit and receive frequencies *of the Coast Station*. We must listen on their transmit frequency and transmit on their receive frequency. It seems obvious, but in the excitement it is all too easy to get them the wrong way round.

It is not possible for two ships to talk to each other on one of the programmed paired frequencies, because they will both be transmitting on the same frequency and both listening on another. For communication between two ships, a simplex channel must be selected. All the distress calling and safety channels are simplex, such as 2182 kHz MF and channel 16 on the VHF.

On the VHF, channel 6 is the primary Inter-ship channel, 13 is for bridge-to-bridge communications, and these too are simplex channels. In the USA, channel 22A is the Coast Guard primary inter-ship simplex channel. If you ever try and talk to the US Coast Guard, they will invariably ask you to switch to 22 Alpha. However, in the rest of the world channel 22 is a duplex channel, so the ship is listening on a different frequency from that on which it is transmitting, so inter-ship communications will not be possible.

Many VHF radios can be switched between the US allocation of channels and the international allocation. It is important to ensure that the appropriate choice of channels is selected for the area where the vessels is operating.

CHAPTER 5

Telex Over Radio

A GMDSS operator is expected to have an idea of how **Telex Over Radio** works, as well as how to use it. We will take a brief look at the technical aspects of telex, then we will look at the actual use and operation of the telex. First of all though, we need to sort out the name. **Telex Over Radio** is sometimes known by its initials, TOR, or because we usually work in **si**mplex mode, SITOR. In the GMDSS regulations it is often referred to as **N**arrow **B**and **D**irect **P**rinting, particularly when it is referring to the Navtex system. Old-timer operators will probably call it RTTY, meaning **R**adio **T**ele-**Ty**pe. As far as we are concerned, it is all the same thing, whatever you choose to call it.

History of Telex

Telex networks on shore began in the late 1920s. The system consisted of a network of cables connecting machines called teleprinters. These were essentially electric typewriters with the keyboard remote from the printer. Two distant machines were connected together, and what was typed on one was printed on the other.

Because it was basically an electro-mechanical system, the speed was limited. An international speed was set at 50 Baud (bits per second), which translates into about 7 letters or numbers per second. This speed is still the present standard, although now with computers sending and receiving the code, very much higher speeds could be achieved. This slow speed has contributed to the almost complete demise of telex ashore.

Afloat though, telex is experiencing a resurgence. Virtually error-free written messages can be transmitted over considerable distances. As we shall see, they can be addressed to 'all ships', a selected group of vessels, or to an individual vessel or coast station. Telex plays a significant role in the GMDSS, as this is how NAVTEX messages are transmitted, and it is in many cases the preferred method of handling emergency traffic, as there is a written record of all transmissions.

Theory of Telex

Telex Over Radio is transmitted using Frequency Shift Keying – the frequency of the carrier wave is switched between two frequencies in a coded pattern. A given pattern of shifts is equivalent to a particular letter.

We can represent the two frequencies as A and Z, and if we were to say that two shifts made up each character, then four coded characters would be possible:

AA, ZZ, AZ and ZA.

If each character was composed of three shifts, then 8 coded characters would be possible:

AAA, ZZZ, AAZ, AZA, ZAA, ZZA, AZZ, ZAZ.

Four shifts would allow 16 characters ($2^4 = 16$), and 5 allows 32 ($2^5=32$). You can either take my word for it, or try writing them out! Being able to send 32 different characters begins to get useful. Twenty-six of these characters can be assigned to letters of the alphabet, with a few left over.

In the early days of terrestrial telex, because of the mechanical nature of the machines five shifts was deemed to be the maximum that was feasible and this has remained the standard ever since. Even a very modest computer now would be able to handle much more complicated series of codes, but back then, five was the limit.

To get round the shortage of characters, to allow all the numbers to be expressed as well as the letters, each combination of shifts is used twice – once for letters and once for numbers. On the old machines, there were two extra keys, one called letter shift and the other figure shift.

When letter shift was pressed, all the following characters were deemed to be letters until figure shift was pressed. Then all the characters that were entered were numbers, or other symbols until the letter shift was pressed again. Fortunately for us, a computer configured to send telex does these shifts for us automatically. All the operator has to do is type, and the computer converts everything to the required shift and code.

This 5-symbol code worked well for terrestrial telex, when, for the most part, the lines were relatively noise free. Trying to use this code over radio proved to be a rather different proposition. The smallest static crash could change a symbol in the code, which would result in the wrong character being received.

41

For example the letter B could be sent – ZAAZZ. A static crash, or other noise might corrupt the first shift, so that AAAZZ is received. This is the code for O. There would be no way that the receiving station could know that it had received the wrong character, so lots of garbled messages could be received.

To solve this problem, two more shifts were added to the code. Seven shifts now gave the possibility of 128 characters ($2^7 = 128$). Of these 128 possible combinations, 35 of them are composed of 3 As and 4 Zs. 93 combinations do not share this characteristic, and are not used. So now it is possible to detect errors caused by the corruption of a single shift. If the received character is not composed of 3 As and 4 Zs, then the receiver knows that there is an error.

In the 7-unit code, B is AZAAZZZ. It has the required 3 As and 4 Zs. If any single one of these is corrupted, there would be too many As or too many Zs and the receiver would know that there is an error.

The system is not absolutely foolproof, because if, for example, both of the first two shifts are corrupted, then ZAAAZZZ would be received. This passes the test for 3 As and 4 Zs, and the error would not be detected, so the character would be read as O.

There are three different protocols that telex can use to try to eliminate errors. The first is called **A**utomatic **R**epeat re**Q**uest. ARQ can only be used when two stations are communicating with each other on a one-to-one basis. Both stations must be capable of transmitting and both must be able to receive.

The station sending the traffic transmits a block of three characters. The receiving station checks that all three characters pass the 3A and 4Z test. If all three characters pass the test, then the receiving station sends a control signal. On receipt of the control signal, the transmitting signal sends the next block of three characters.

There are two control signals, 1 and 2, and each time the receiving station receives a block of three characters that pass the test, it alternates control signals. So on receiving the second block of characters correctly, the receiving station transmits control signal 2. If the next block is also received correctly, it sends control signal 1, and so on.

If a block of three is received which does not pass the 3 As, 4 Zs test, then the receiving station repeats the last control signal used. The transmitting station automatically repeats the same block of three characters. If it is correctly received, then the receiving station transmits the alternate control signal and the transmitting station sends the next block. If it is still received as an error, the receiving station continues to repeat the last control signal until the block is correctly received. A block can be attempted up to 32 times before the transmitting station gives up and restarts the link.

The second protocol is called **Forward Error Correction**. FEC does not require the receiving station to transmit, so it can be used to send messages to a number of vessels at the same time. This is the protocol that is used for sending traffic lists, distress, urgency and safety messages. This is also the method that is used for NAVTEX, which is in effect **N**arrow **B**and **D**irect **P**rinting messages being transmitted to all stations.

When using FEC, the transmitting station sends each character twice with a short pause between. The receiving station checks the first character for 3 As and 4 Zs. If it passes the test, it is printed and the repeat character is ignored.

However, if the first character fails the test, then the receiver looks at the repeat of the character. If the repeat passes the test, then it gets printed. If it too fails the test, then usually a * is printed to mark the corrupt character, and the receiver moves on to the next character.

The third protocol is **SEL**ective **F**orward **E**rror **C**orrection. SELFEC operates in a similar manner to FEC but it is designed for sending a message to just one station, who, perhaps because they are in harbour, cannot transmit, and so cannot receive a message by ARQ.

As in FEC, each character is transmitted twice, so the receiving station has two chances at receiving it correctly. However, the beginning of the message contains the SELCALL number of the receiving station, and this alerts the receiver to the fact that it is about to receive a SELFEC message. The transmitting station then inverts all the shifts, so each character is now made up of 4 As and 3 Zs. Any other receiver which is picking up the message will reject it, but the intended receiver, after it has been warned to expect a SELFEC message, inverts all the shifts before it begins to de-code the message. The received characters now appear to be composed of 3 As and 4 Zs, and can be read as normal.

Using Telex

Every telex station, whether on a ship or on shore has an address and an answerback code. The exchange of answerback codes ensures that you are in contact with the correct station.

The address for shore-based subscribers is a number, just like a telephone number. The only slightly confusing thing is that the international country codes for telex subscribers use different numbers than are used for telephone calls, so care is needed to ensure that you are calling the correct country if you are sending an international telex. The answerback code for a shore station is the telex number followed by a group of letters (often a part of the company name), then a letter indicating the country e.g. 123456 BOATS G.

43

The address for a ship station is a five-digit **Selective Calling** number and that for a Coast Station is a four-digit Selcall number. For ship stations the answerback consists of the ship's Selcall number followed by the call sign and the letter X e.g. 98765 GABC X. A Coast Station will have an answerback consisting of its Selcall number, some arrangement of letters, followed by the country letter of identification.

Telex traffic can be sent 'direct', in which case the ship station and the shore subscriber are in direct contact, and can exchange messages virtually instantaneously, or the message can be sent as 'store and forward'. With a store and forward telex, the message is stored in a computer at the shore station and forwarded to the recipient as and when that becomes possible.

Most Coast Stations are equipped to deal automatically with telex traffic, so you are working with a computer rather than an operator. The computer will recognise a series of codes, so you can tell it what sort of service you want. Many of the codes are standardised, and the appropriate list of radio signals will either itemise any unusual procedure, or give you an access code which will tell the computer at the Coast Station to send you a list of their operating codes.

Under GMDSS, initial contact with the Coast Station will be by **Digital Selective Calling**. The DSC acknowledgement from the Coast Station will give details of the working channel to be used. It will be a pair of frequencies. If the MF/HF radio cannot accept a given ITU channel, then the receive and transmit frequencies must be entered into the radio. Care must be taken to get these the right way round. You must listen on their transmit frequency and transmit on their receive frequency.

A full list of the telex service codes can be found in the appropriate list of radio signals, or on request from the particular Coast Station. The most important codes are:

TLX	'Store and forward' telex service – the message is stored at the Coast Station to be forwarded later
DIRTLX	Direct telex service – two-way communications
MSG+	To receive messages which are stored for the ship
SVC+	Message for the Coast Station
URG+	Connects to an operator to request urgent safety assistance
MED+	Request for medical advice
OPR+	Operator assistance
HELP+	Request for list of procedures and facilities available
GA+?	Go Ahead – invitation to transmit
KKKK	End communication with a subscriber on a direct link
BRK+	End communication with the Coast Station

Once a channel has been assigned by DSC, telex contact can be made with the Coast Station by calling them on the designated frequency. Remember to use ARQ mode since you are communicating one-to-one. The Coast Station's call is the four-digit Selcall number, which is normally the same as the last four digits as the MMSI for the station. (The allocation of **Maritime Mobile Service Identities** is covered in Chapter 10.)

The station will respond with its answerback and will automatically request the ship station's answerback. Most modern telex units will automatically send it on request, but there are some which require it to be sent by pressing a key. On receipt of your answerback code, the Coast Station will send GA+?, which is your invitation to transmit.

If you want to check for any messages, send MSG+. If there are any messages they will be sent, and if there are none the Coast Station will say 'no traffic', or something similar, and then send GA+? again.

If you have a message to send, select the service you require using one of the codes above. For example to send a 'store and forward' telex to a national number, e.g. 123456, key in: TLX123456+.

As soon as the Coast Station is ready to receive the message it will send MSG+? Which is your signal to send the message. Your message should finish with KKKK to let the Coast Station know that the message is ended. The Coast Station will exchange answerbacks with you again, and send GA+? If you have more traffic, repeat the procedure. When you have no more traffic, then send BRK+ to terminate the connection with the Coast Station.

The procedure for opening a direct telex contact is similar, except that you precede the number with DIRTLX, and once contact is established with the subscriber, it is normal to exchange answerbacks with them, at the beginning and at the end of the contact. KKKK will terminate the contact with the subscriber, but keep the link open with the Coast Station if you want to send further traffic. When you send KKKK the Coast Station will reply to you with a GA+?, at which point you can dial another DIRTLX, or other service. If you have no further traffic, then BRK+ will close the link with the Coast Station.

The commands used by various Coast Stations are by no means universal. Some require all commands to terminate with '+?' While others only require '+'. Also, when placing international calls through a Coast Station, some require the country code to be preceded by 00 while others use just 0. (Once again, remember that the telex country code is different to the telephone country code.)

It is good practice to look up the Coast Station in a list of radio signals before trying to operate with them, particularly for the first time. Many times their required codes will be listed, or a code will be given to access their 'Help' message which will list all of their operating codes.

45

When sending a distress, urgency or safety message by telex, the message should start with:

- at least one carriage return
- one line feed
- one letter shift
- then the appropriate emergency signal, i.e. Mayday (or, if you can remember, it should be SOS on telex) for a distress message, or, Pan Pan for an urgency message, or, *Securité* for a safety message.

Remember to include your identity, and if it is a distress situation your position and the nature of your distress. Finish your message with GA+? to tell the Coast Station or RCC that you have finished that particular transmission and are standing by to receive their answer.

The ITU suggests that whenever possible distress working is conducted by telex, so that there is a written copy of all transmissions available. Obviously, if time is short, your vessel is sinking and you are a slow typist, then voice communication may well be preferable!

A vessel not equipped with DSC, wanting to send a telex via a Coast Station will have to call them directly on a working channel. Select a suitable channel, which will be a pair of frequencies, and listen to ensure that the channel is not already being used by another vessel. Many Coast Stations transmit their call sign in Morse code on any channels which are available for use. If the channel is in use passing telex traffic, you will hear the characteristic regular chirping sound of an ARQ transmission. If the channel is clear, call the Coast Station, giving your Selcall number. The Coast Station should reply and then the procedure is the same as above.

CHAPTER 6

Digital Selective Calling

Digital Selective Calling is the fundamental reason why the GMDSS system is different from what has been available until now.

Prior to DSC, most radio calls were initiated by making a voice call to the desired station, and relying on somebody at that station hearing the call and then responding to it. All too often the sheer volume of calls made this an impossible task. On a summer afternoon in popular sailing areas it was not unusual for there to be over 400 calls per hour on VHF channel 16. At best, this made it very tedious, and often impossible, to hear calls meant for you, or more importantly, for anybody to hear a distress call. Clearly, something had to be done.

Initially a partial answer was found by shifting some of the calling traffic off channel 16. In some areas Coast Stations stopped monitoring channel 16 and listened for calls only on their working channels. Similarly, calls to marinas were stopped on 16 and moved to other designated channels. That relieved some of the pressure, but now there was no single channel that everybody was listening to, so vessels missed calls meant for them and distress calls sometimes went unheeded.

On board commercial ships, the problem was even worse. They were not only expected to monitor channel 16, but also 13 for bridge-to-bridge calls, 2182 MHz on MF, and if on the high seas, one or more HF distress frequencies. What a headache – literally!

The salvation lay in DSC. The DSC control unit monitors all the required frequencies, and lets the operator know when there is a call for his station, or when there is a distress or other urgent call. Best of all, it does all this in total silence. No longer are we subjected to the continuous cacophony on channel 16 nor the static crashes and bangs on 2182 MHz. Instead, we wait for the phone to ring, as it were.

47

How DSC Works

How is this miracle achieved? As was explained in the introduction, the DSC control unit is somewhat like a pager which alerts the receiving station that there is traffic waiting for them. The name, **Digital Selective Calling**, goes a long way to explaining how it works.

DSC uses a **Digital** signal to send a message, via the sending station's radio, to alert the receiver that there is traffic for them, and to tell them where and how to receive the traffic. This DSC message is termed a DSC Call, or sometimes a DSC Alert. The digital message includes several pieces of information which will be displayed on the receiving station's DSC control unit:

1. The **Maritime Mobile Service Identity** of the sending station. The MMSI is a nine digit number, and it is the DSC equivalent to the call sign, or the 'phone number' of a station. It is issued as part of the GMDSS station licence.
2. The MMSI of the station being called. This can be an individual vessel or Coast Station, a specific group of vessels, or in the case of distress, urgency or safety traffic, to all stations.
3. The priority of the call – distress, urgency, safety or routine. DSC can be used for setting up any type of call, from a Mayday to making a phone call home to say that the fishing is good, and you will be late for supper.
4. For distress calls, the DSC alert can include the nature of the distress, e.g. fire, sinking, explosion, pirate attack etc.
5. For distress calls the position of the vessel is normally included. If the control unit is interfaced to a **Global Positioning System** receiver, then the position will be added automatically. If there is no GPS receiver connected to it, then the position, and the time that the position was valid, must be keyed in.
6. The requested working frequency and mode of transmission for the traffic. The DSC is only used to set up the call; the actual communication is conducted on another radio channel – distress or working channel as the case may be – and it can be conducted in either voice or telex mode, depending on circumstances.

DSC calls are **Selective**, because as we have seen above, they can be directed to a selected station or stations. Previously virtually all calls were received by all stations who were in range of the transmission. However, the DSC control unit looks at each call that it receives and determines if the call is addressed to it specifically, to it as part of a group, to all stations, or to vessels in the area where the receiving station is located. When such a call is received then the operator is alerted, usually by a buzzer and an indication on the screen. The information as to where and how the traffic will be sent is displayed on the screen. All other calls are simply ignored.

The last part of the name sums up what DSC is about. It is used for **Calling** another station to advise them that there is traffic for them, and to what channel or frequency they should tune their radio to receive this traffic.

When a DSC call is transmitted by VHF, it is sent in F1B modulation, at a speed of 1,200 baud. At this speed, all the data in a DSC Alert can be transmitted in about half a second. On MF/HF things happen just a little slower. The modulation is J2B and the speed of transmission is 100 baud. This results in a DSC Alert on MF or HF taking between 6 and 7 seconds to be transmitted. The DSC control unit transmits the DSC calls through the ship's VHF and/or MF/HF radio. Although installations and equipment obviously vary, the control unit is normally also connected to a dedicated receiver which monitors the DSC frequencies for incoming DSC calls, regardless of to which frequencies the ship's radios are tuned.

Now, let's take a look at the DSC operation and procedures for VHF, MF and HF radios.

A pair of Inmarsat B antennae – the twin large domes.

CHAPTER 7

Radio Procedures Using DSC

Radios on board a vessel can be used to communicate with other vessels or with a variety of shore stations. They can be used for transmitting distress, urgency, and safety messages, as well as for what is termed routine traffic. The use of marine radios is supposed to be restricted to ship business, and the passing of telephone traffic via a commercial Coast Station. A marine radio is not meant to be used for idle chit-chat. CB radios and mobile phones exist for that purpose.

Whether or not you need an operator licence and/or a ship station licence depends on the administration under whose flag your vessel is operating and on the country in whose waters you are located. In the UK, both an operator licence and a ship station licence is required for all UK flag vessels and for all vessels operating in UK waters. In the USA, private vessels up to 20 metres being operated purely for pleasure do not require a licence to operate a VHF radio, provided they are not trying to communicate with a foreign station. A ship station licence and an operator licence are needed for vessels over 20 metres, vessels carrying passengers, or to use an MF/HF radio.

Inter-ship communications are not normally permitted when a vessel is inside, or within a mile, of any harbour, port, dock or anchorage, except in the case of distress, an emergency involving danger to life or danger to navigation or by the Port Operations Service. An exception is usually granted on inland waterways when inter-ship communications are permitted, provided both vessels are underway. In many countries, vessels in port are allowed to exchange communications through the nearest Coast Station within that country, to make telephone calls.

Theoretically, under GMDSS all initial contacts are to be made by DSC on specific DSC frequencies. The DSC control unit uses the ship's radio to transmit a DSC call, either to a particular vessel or Coast Station, to a group of vessels, perhaps in a specific area, or in the case of distress, to all stations. Once the receiving station has been alerted by DSC that there is traffic then the messages are passed by voice or by telex on other appropriate frequencies on VHF, MF or HF.

VHF, MF and HF all have specific channels or frequencies allocated for particular purposes, be it for DSC calling, emergency communications or the passing of routine traffic. On VHF we normally refer to channels rather than to specific frequencies. On MF and HF there is a list of International Telecommunication Union channels, to which some Coast Stations will refer, but very often frequencies are given rather than a channel number.

The DSC emergency calling frequencies are:

VHF– Channel 70 (also used for routine calls)
MF – 2187.5 kHz
HF – 4207.5 kHz. 6312 kHz. 8414.5 kHz. 12577 kHz. 16804.5 kHz.

The frequencies for transmission of emergency messages by *voice* are:

VHF– Channel 16
MF – 2182 kHz
HF – 4125 kHz. 6215 kHz. 8291 kHz. 12290 kHz. 16420 kHz.

The frequencies for transmission of emergency messages by *telex* are:

VHF– Not applicable.
MF – 2174.5 kHz
HF – 4177.5 kHz. 6268 kHz. 8376.5 kHz. 12520 kHz. 16695 kHz

Many channels, both on VHF and on MF/HF, are so-called duplex channels, where a station transmits on one frequency and receives on another. Such pairing of frequencies is normal for those channels used for communication between a vessel and a Coast Station for traffic such as telephone calls. With suitable radio equipment, this pairing of frequencies allows a normal conversation to take place just as over an ordinary telephone. On a full duplex link either party can hear the other talk, even when they themselves are talking. But, when a single frequency is used for both transmitting and receiving, then each station must take turns to talk while the other listens. In this situation, one person says 'Over' when they have finished speaking, and this is the signal for the other person to speak. It is not normally possible for two ships to talk to each other on a duplex channel, because they will both be transmitting on one frequency and both listening on the other. For inter-ship communications, a simplex channel must be used.

51

Operating a VHF Radio

The controls on a VHF radio set are extremely simple. The basic controls consist of a volume control, which often incorporates the on/off switch, a control for selecting the channel, and a squelch control. The squelch is used to suppress noise interference. With the volume set at about mid-point, the squelch control should be turned down until the noise of interference is heard. The control should then be turned up until the noise just stops. The set is then ready to operate. If the squelch is not adjusted correctly and it is set too high, weak signals will be suppressed as well as the noise and calls for the vessel could be missed. There may also be a 'dual watch' switch. When this is operated, it allows the distress channel 16 to be monitored as well as another frequency.

The situation on VHF is slightly complicated by the fact that the USA uses a different channel allocation to the rest of the world. Many VHF sets can be switched from one standard to the other, and if a vessel is planning to move in and out of the USA, then such a set would be vital. A list of the channels and frequencies for both standards is included in the Appendix.

Fortunately for all concerned, the most important VHF channels are the same under both systems.

Channel 70 – DSC distress and calling frequency. This channel is only for DSC calling – no voice communications are allowed on this channel. This is the VHF channel that a DSC-equipped vessel should monitor.

Channel 16 – This is the pre-DSC distress and calling channel. For non-DSC equipped vessels, this is still the channel to be monitored. Channel 16 must not be used for holding conversations. It is reserved for emergency traffic and for making contact only. All other conversations must be conducted on another channel.

Channel 9 – In many areas, including the East Coast of the USA and most of Europe, except for the UK, this is the secondary calling channel. Marinas and yacht harbours will often monitor channel 9 to decrease the amount of traffic on channel 16. However, in the UK channel 9 is for the use of pilot vessels and tugs and channel 80 is allocated as the marina channel.

Channel 6 – This is the primary inter-ship channel. Whatever channels a VHF radio may or may not have, in addition to channel 16, every radio should have channel 6. This is classed as a safety channel, and so it is not a channel to use for prolonged conversations, but it can be used for passing safety messages.

Channel 13 – This is used for inter-ship communications concerning navigation or safety. If you want to confirm a particular manoeuvre with another vessel, then this is the channel to use. Channel 13 is designated for bridge-to-bridge communications under GMDSS.

Channels 8 and 72 – These are inter-ship channels on both the International and USA systems and can be used for routine traffic between vessels.

Most VHF radios have a high power and a low power setting. For a fixed station (as opposed to a handheld), the high power is normally 25 watts, which is the maximum output power allowed on VHF and the low power is about 1 watt. It is good practice to use the low power setting whenever possible so as not to interfere with other vessels who may be communicating with each other a few miles away. In distress conditions always use high power. Indeed some sets cannot be switched to low power on channel 16.

Operating an MF/HF Radio

Vessels operating in A2 areas, that is beyond the range of VHF Coast Stations, can use Medium Frequency radio for making distress, urgency, safety, and routine calls. Normally MF is used up to a range of about a hundred miles. Greater distances are possible, especially at night, but generally High Frequency will be used for longer ranges. Normally the MF transmitter/receiver is combined with the HF radio – a purely MF radio is rare.

The controls on an MF/HF transceiver vary greatly from one make to another and operators should take time to become familiar with the particular set that they will be using. However, there are some controls which are basic to all sets:

Volume – Sometimes called Audio Frequency control. This sets the volume of the signal that you are hearing.

Radio Frequency – This sets the level of the incoming signal. If the signal is too strong, it will be distorted. The RF control should be set as high as possible without distorting the signal.

Automatic Gain Control – The AGC will keep adjusting the level of the incoming signal to a constant level. It is normally an on/off switch. Under most conditions it is best to use the radio with the AGC on, in which case the RF control should be set at maximum.

Tune – For MF or HF operations the antenna must be tuned to resonate at the frequency being used. Most modern sets use an automatic tuner. Tuning is simply a case of selecting the frequency and pressing the tune button. If there is not an automatic tuner, then the operator must learn how to manually tune the antenna. Any tuning must be done at low power, and wherever possible, using a dummy antenna to minimise interference with other stations.

Frequency – Most modern radios offer the choice of selecting an ITU channel, or an individual frequency or pair of frequencies. Using an ITU channel will set the correct frequency for receive and transmit. If the operator chooses to input

53

the frequencies directly, then care must be taken when using a duplex pair of frequencies that they are put in the right way round, i.e. you are not transmitting where you should be listening.

Clarifier – If the received signal is difficult to hear and sounds as if it is not on the correct frequency, then try adjusting the clarifier. This control actually adjusts the oscillator which is re-inserting the carrier, but it has the effect of fine tuning the receiver frequency.

Mode – This determines the modulation of emissions that the radio will transmit and receive. Normal marine voice communications are J3E (SSB – suppressed carrier 'Just the sideband'). Other options may be H3E which was used on 2182 kHz pre-GMDSS (SSB with full carrier – 'wHole carrier') and A3E (double sideband – 'All the components'). This is AM modulation of commercial medium wave broadcasts. If the radio is equipped to send and receive telex, then there should be a position on the mode switch for telex and this could be marked J2B or FSK, or even RTTY. It is important that the correct modulation is set, otherwise the signals will neither be transmitted nor received properly.

2182 – Most radios give an instant access to the International Distress Frequency of 2182 kHz. Pre GMDSS, all transmissions on 2182 kHz were made on H3E, (SSB with 'wHole carrier'), but this requirement has gone, and under GMDSS all SSB transmissions should be J3E (suppressed carrier – 'Just the sideband').

We need to consider distress, urgency, safety and routine calls. Using DSC, the procedures are similar whether using VHF, MF or HF. There are some differences, mainly because of the differing nature of propagation between the three types of radio. We will look at the four different types of calls in turn, starting with distress calls.

Transmitting, Receiving and Relaying Distress, Urgency and Safety Calls

Distress Calls

We must remember that a distress call should only be made when a vessel or person is in grave *and* imminent danger. (Under GMDSS a person overboard is a distress situation, before GMDSS this was classed as an urgency situation.) If the danger is not grave *and* imminent, then an urgency call should be made instead. A distress call should only be made on the direct orders of the Master.

With distress calls, we need to know:

1. How to send a distress alert
2. What to do if we receive a distress alert
3. How to relay a distress call from another vessel
4. What to do if we hear a distress call being relayed.

1. *Transmission of a Distress Alert*

Although equipment varies, the DSC control unit will have a distress button clearly labelled, and normally protected by a safety flap. To send a distress alert:

a. Press the distress button to initiate the distress mode.
b. Select the band on which the alert is to be transmitted, VHF, MF, or one of the HF bands.
c. The radio must be tuned to the DSC distress channel of the chosen band. The DSC control unit may do this automatically, but if not, then it must be done manually.
e. If time allows, key in or select from the on-screen menu, the nature of the distress, the vessel's position (if it is not automatically included from a GPS receiver) and the time in UTC when the position was valid.
e. If time allows, key in or select the nature of the distress, e.g. grounding, abandon ship, fire, piracy attack etc.
f. Select type of subsequent communication – voice or telex, and the frequency to be used.
g. Transmit the distress alert – usually by a second prolonged push of the distress button or by pushing another button, depending on the equipment.
h. Prepare for the subsequent traffic by tuning the radio to the emergency frequency of the band used to transmit the alert. Many DSC control units will do this automatically.

The receiver for the DSC control unit will continue to monitor the DSC channels for the reception of a DSC distress acknowledgement. For alerts sent by VHF or MF, if the DSC control unit can automatically tune the radio to the correct frequency, it will repeat the transmission of the distress alert at about four-minute intervals until it receives a DSC acknowledgement or the operator cancels the alert. If the radio has to be manually tuned, then any repeat alerts will have to be sent manually by repeating the above steps.

On HF, the propagation conditions between the various bands vary greatly. Transmission on more than one HF band will increase the chance of it being received by a Coast Station. This can be achieved in one of two ways:

1. Transmit the distress alert twice, on one HF band, with a 45-second gap. This gives the best chance for a scanning receiver to receive the alert. Then wait a few minutes to see if it is acknowledged by a Coast Station. If there is no DSC acknowledgement received within 3 minutes, switch to another HF band and try again. This process is repeated until a DSC acknowledgement is received.
2. Most DSC control units will allow you to make a series of distress alerts, on several or all of the HF bands, with little or no pause between them. The operator then watches to see on which band the DSC acknowledgement is received and then proceeds accordingly.

If time permits, the first method, a systematic attempt on the most likely bands, will usually make it easier to find and select the best band for the working of the distress traffic. Which frequency is chosen obviously depends upon the anticipated propagation between the calling station and the desired Coast Station. Under many conditions 8414.5 kHz is a good one with which to start. If it is daylight, and the Coast Station is far away, a higher frequency might be better. At night, or if the vessel is close to an A2 area, then a lower frequency could be more suitable. Whichever band permits the DSC alert to be received is likely to support the distress traffic.

However, if time is short, then the so-called 'multi-hit' method gives the best chance of having at least the alert picked up. Even if there is no time to follow up the alert with any distress traffic, if the alert has been sent properly the Coast Station will have your identity, the fact that you are in distress, the nature of the distress and your position. Even if they cannot establish voice or telex contact, the alert should be enough to initiate search and rescue.

When sending an HF DSC alert, if time permits, an MF and VHF DSC alert should be sent as well to alert any vessels that may be in the area but which will not hear the HF alert because of the skip zone.

While waiting for a DSC acknowledgement, you should also listen on the emergency frequency of the band on which the alert was transmitted for any vessels acknowledging reception of the alert by voice. When a DSC acknowledgement is received, or if any station is heard acknowledging the alert on the emergency frequency, transmit the distress message.

TRANSMISSION OF THE DISTRESS MESSAGE

The ITU recommend that telex is used for distress traffic wherever possible because there is a written copy of all communications, but if time is short, voice may be quicker.

Tune the radio to the voice or telex emergency frequency of the band on which the alert was transmitted or the band on which an acknowledgement was received.

Voice emergency frequencies are:

VHF– Channel 16
MF – 2182 kHz
HF – 4125 kHz. 6215 kHz. 8291 kHz. 12290 kHz. 16420 kHz.

Telex emergency frequencies are:

VHF– Not applicable.
MF – 2174.5 kHz
HF – 4177.5 kHz. 6268 kHz. 8376.5 kHz. 12520 kHz. 16695 kHz

A distress message is the only type of traffic that does not have to be addressed to somebody. A distress message is 'broadcast' to anybody who may be listening.

Any distress message should follow the standard format, using the mnemonic MIPDANIO.

Mayday – Mayday indicates that it is a distress message. Under GMDSS there is no need to repeat the 'Mayday' three times as we did before GMDSS. That is the call and the call has already been made by DSC.

Identity – This is ……….. Your MMSI number, repeated three times. This is the only identification known to other stations who have received the DSC call. If there is time, the call sign and name of your vessel can be included.

Position – This may have been included in the DSC alert, but should be given again. In coastal waters a range and bearing from a prominent feature may mean more to receiving stations than a latitude and longitude from the GPS

Distress – The nature of the distress, e.g. aground, sinking, pirate attack etc.

Assistance requested – For example, need help abandoning ship, or a tow off a lee shore etc.

Number of people on board – It is useful for rescuers to know how many people are to be rescued, so that they know what sort of vessel to send and how many people they must search for in the case of an abandoned vessel.

Information – Any other information which will help the rescuers, e.g. wind and sea conditions, visibility, numbers of injured persons etc.

Over – Terminate the transmission with the MMSI number and/or call sign and name of the vessel and the word 'over', so that other stations know that the transmission has ended, and they may reply. Remember to release the key on the microphone, otherwise you will not be able to hear any reply.

If the 'MIPDANIO' format is followed, you are sure to send all the required information at the first attempt, and if for some reason the message cannot be completed, then the most important bits have been sent first.

On MF or HF, if transmitting the Distress Message by voice select J3E mode. If the distress traffic is to be conducted on telex, unless otherwise instructed by a Coast Station use the **Forward Error Correction** mode. FEC allows other stations to copy the traffic, as well as the station for whom it is intended. Start the transmission with at least one carriage return, a line feed, a letter shift and either the word Mayday, or SOS.

2. Reception of a Distress Alert

A vessel receiving a DSC distress alert should *not* normally acknowledge the alert by DSC, but should do so by voice or telex on the emergency frequency indicated in the alert. A DSC acknowledgement is usually done only by a

Coast Station, because acknowledging the alert by DSC will stop the transmitting station from sending further alerts. Generally, it is much better for all concerned if a Coast Station hears and acknowledges the alert, and then assumes control of the operation.

Another vessel should only acknowledge the alert by DSC if it is being transmitted on VHF or MF, and if it seems that no Coast Station has received the call and the transmission of the distress alert is continuing. In this situation, the receiving vessel may acknowledge the call by DSC to terminate the transmissions. But the receiving vessel is then required to contact the nearest Coast Station by any practical means and inform them of the situation.

A DSC distress alert on HF should *never* be acknowledged by DSC by another vessel, because by the nature of HF propagation the two vessels are likely to be many hundreds of miles apart. Transmission of a DSC acknowledgement will stop the transmission of further alerts, and it would be better for the distressed vessel to continue sending alerts in the hope that a Coast Station will receive the call directly and take control of the situation. A vessel receiving an alert on HF should relay the alert to a Coast Station.

RECEPTION OF A DSC DISTRESS ALERT ON VHF OR MF

If a DSC distress alert is received on VHF or MF, the normal procedure to follow is:

a. Watch the DSC control unit for reception of a DSC acknowledgement from a Coast Station. Such an acknowledgement will stop further transmissions of the distress alert.
b. Tune the radio to the frequency and mode indicated in the DSC alert.
c. Acknowledge the receipt of the distress alert on the frequency indicated, either by voice or by telex as indicated in the DSC alert.

The message acknowledging the distress alert should be as follows:

Mayday – The word Mayday indicates that it is a distress message.

Identity of Distressed *vessel.* – This will be their MMSI, repeated three times – neither the name nor the call sign of the distressed vessel will be indicated on the DSC alert.

This is......... – Your identity – your MMSI and/or name and call sign, repeated three times.

Received Mayday.

Over.

If there is a Coast Station, or **R**escue **C**o-ordination **C**entre controlling the operation and they want you to help, they will call you back. If no Coast Station nor RCC has taken control, the distressed vessel should hear your acknowledgement and may call you back to ask for your assistance if it is needed. If no Coast Station nor RCC has taken control and you do not hear any response to your acknowledgement by the distressed vessel, then you should send a distress alert relay.

Reception of a Distress Alert on HF

Vessels operating in Areas A3 and A4 are expected to monitor at least two of the DSC HF emergency frequencies. Normally 8414.5 kHz is designated as one and the other is chosen according to conditions – a lower frequency by night or a higher one by day. Many DSC watch-keeping receivers will in fact scan through all the DSC emergency frequencies, which are:

4207.5 kHz.   6312 kHz.   8414.5 kHz.   12577 kHz.   16804.5 kHz

If you receive a DSC distress alert on HF from another ship you must *not* acknowledge it by DSC. Because of the likely propagation of the HF signal it is probable that the other vessel is several hundreds, or possibly thousands of miles away. If the distress alert was acknowledged by DSC then no further distress alerts would be transmitted by the distressed station, and this could well reduce the chances of it being heard by a shore station who could co-ordinate rescue attempts.

If you do receive an HF DSC distress alert then the correct procedure is:

a. Note on which band or bands the DSC alert was received.
b. Note the position of the distressed vessel, and compare to your own. Unless the HF signal was received on ground wave, it is likely to be many hundreds of miles from your own position.
c. Tune the HF radio to the mode and frequency indicated in the alert, or if no frequency and mode was specified then to the emergency frequency in the band on which the DSC alert was received. The HF emergency frequencies are:
Voice emergency frequencies:

4125 kHz.   6215 kHz.   8291 kHz.   12290 kHz.   16420 kHz.

Telex emergency frequencies:

4177.5 kHz.   6268 kHz.   8376.5 kHz.   12520 kHz.   16695 kHz

If telex was specified in the alert then the telex frequency should be monitored, but if it is possible to monitor the voice frequency on the same band as well then this should be done. If the DSC alert was received on several frequencies then monitor the most likely band, probably 8 MHz if the alert was received on this band.
d. If no distress traffic is heard on the frequency to which you tuned within two minutes, then switch to the emergency frequency on another band on which the DSC alert was received or another of the emergency frequencies that might be

appropriate, considering the position of the other vessel in relation to you and the likely propagation.

e. If distress working is heard, then the situation should be monitored until it is obvious that the Coast Station has the situation under control. If no distress working is heard and no DSC acknowledgement has been transmitted by a Coast Station, then transmit a DSC distress alert relay to inform the nearest **R**escue Co-ordination **C**entre or Coast Station by any means possible.

3. *Transmission of a Distress Alert Relay*

A vessel should transmit a distress alert relay if:

a. the distressed vessel herself is not able to transmit a distress alert.
b. the master of the relaying ship considers that more assistance is required.
c. a distress alert has been received but no contact with the distressed vessel has been possible and no Coast Station has responded to the alert.

The distress alert relay could be sent to 'all stations', to vessels in a particular area or to a specific Coast Station or RCC. On VHF or MF an 'all stations' call might be considered appropriate to alert vessels in the vicinity as well as any Coast Stations within range. Usually, in the case of an HF DSC alert relay, it will be better to send it to a specific Coast Station or **R**escue Co-ordination **C**entre, and let them co-ordinate the rescue. Do not do an 'all stations' call. There is no point in alerting vessels, for example, in the Indian Ocean for a vessel in distress in the North Atlantic.

A DSC distress alert relay is sent as follows.

a. Tune the radio to the DSC emergency frequency of the most suitable band.
b. Select 'distress relay' on the DSC control unit.
c. Address the call as 'all stations', or to the MMSI of a specific Coast Station or RCC.
d. Key in the MMSI of the distressed vessel, if known.
e. Select the nature of the distress, if known.
f. Key in position of distressed vessel.
g. Key in UTC time that the position was valid.
h. Indicate frequency and mode for subsequent traffic.
i. Transmit the DSC distress alert relay.
j. Watch on the DSC control unit for a DSC acknowledgement. Tune the radio to the stipulated frequency and mode, and transmit the distress relay message.

The distress relay message should take the format:

Mayday relay – Mayday indicates that there is a distress situation, but by adding the word 'relay' it indicates at once that it is not you in distress.

This is......... – Your MMSI, name of vessel, and call sign.

Text of message – Indicating identity and position of distressed vessel, nature of distress, assistance needed and number of persons on board if known.

4. Reception of a Distress Alert Relay

When a Coast Station, RCC, or indeed another vessel, has received, and acknowledged a DSC distress alert it may elect to transmit a distress alert relay to other vessels. It can do this to all stations, a group of vessels, vessels in a particular geographic area, or to one specific vessel. Vessels receiving such a DSC alert should *not* acknowledge it by DSC, but instead should tune to the indicated frequency and mode and acknowledge it on the appropriate frequency on the same band as it was received. The procedure is:

a. Do *not* acknowledge by DSC. Tune the radio to the appropriate frequency and mode indicated in the relay call.
b. Acknowledge the alert relay by voice or telex as appropriate.

The format of the acknowledgement message is:

Mayday – The word Mayday indicates that it is a distress message.

Identity of Distressed *vessel* – This will be their MMSI, repeated three times. (Neither the name nor the call sign of the distressed vessel will have been indicated on the DSC alert.

This is......... – Your identity, including your MMSI and/or name and call sign, repeated three times.

Received Mayday.

Over.

If there is a Coast Station or **R**escue **C**o-ordination **C**entre controlling the operation and they want you to help, they will call you back. Continue to monitor the frequency after you have transmitted the acknowledgement.

If a DSC distress alert relay is received from another ship who has perhaps done an 'all stations' distress alert relay, the procedure is exactly the same. Do not acknowledge by DSC, instead acknowledge by voice or telex as appropriate, in exactly the same way as above.

Urgency Calls

An urgency call is for serious situations but not one where the ship or a person is in 'grave *and* imminent' danger. An example of an urgency call might be a vessel which has lost her engines and may be swept ashore in the next hour or so. The danger is grave, but not yet imminent, so the correct call is an urgency call rather than a distress call. A serious medical problem may warrant an urgency call for assistance or evacuation. An urgency call must not be broadcast to the world in general, it must be addressed to somebody, even if it is to 'all stations.'

Transmission of an Urgency Alert

DSC is used to alert other stations that an urgency message is about to be transmitted on a nominated frequency. The message itself is then transmitted on an appropriate frequency in the normal way. The procedure is:

a. Select 'urgency call' on the DSC control unit.
b. Select on which band you want to transmit the DSC alert.
c. Tune the radio to the DSC frequency of the chosen band. The DSC control unit may do this for you.
d. Address the call to 'all stations' or to the MMSI of a particular Coast Station or vessel, or group of vessels.
e. Key in the mode and frequency on which the urgency message will be transmitted.
f. Transmit the DSC urgency alert.

Transmission of an Urgency Message

The radio can now be tuned to the emergency frequency of the band on which the DSC alert was sent for transmission of the urgency message.

The format of an urgency message is:

Pan Pan – The words Pan Pan indicate that the message is an urgency message, and as such, it should have priority over all but distress traffic. In the case of a request for medical assistance, the signal is Pan Pan Medico. Note that this is for medical assistance. A request for medical advice is not a Pan Pan.

Address – All messages except distress must be addressed to somebody. A general call, perhaps for a tow, would be addressed to 'all stations'. A Pan Pan Medico is more likely to be addressed to a specific Coast Station, but under some circumstances that too could be addressed to 'all stations'.

Identity – You must identify yourself in all transmissions. Any station that has received your urgency call on DSC has received your MMSI number as part of the call, so your identity should include the MMSI number as well as the name and call-sign of your vessel.

Position – This may have been included in the DSC call, but it should be repeated here. If somebody is to help you, they need to know where you are. As in the distress message, your position as a distance and bearing from a prominent landmark may mean more to the receiving station than a latitude and longitude.

Assistance – State what assistance is needed.

Over – Terminate the message with Pan Pan, name of your vessel and call-sign, and the word 'over', so the other stations know you have finished, and they can respond.

Once communications have been established with a suitable station, the subsequent traffic will normally transfer off the emergency frequency onto a working channel. If the communication is on VHF and the traffic is inter-ship, then channel 6 could be used. If the communication is with the Coastguard, then they will probably transfer operations to channel 67 in the UK or 22A in the USA. A Coast Station will move communications to one of their working channels.

Reception of an Urgency Alert

Vessels receiving a DSC urgency alert should *not* acknowledge by DSC but should switch to the indicated channel, normally the emergency frequency for the band where the DSC alert was received, and listen for the urgency message.

Safety Calls

A safety call is to warn other vessels of a particular danger. It may be some danger to navigation, such as a drifting derelict or it could be an urgent weather warning. Again, the call and the message must be addressed to somebody even if it is to 'all stations'. The DSC safety alert can be addressed to 'all stations', a particular Coast Station, a group of vessels, vessels in a specified geographic area, or an individual vessel.

Safety messages if they are short (less than a minute in duration), and if they are primarily intended for vessels in the immediate vicinity can be transmitted on the emergency frequency, but any longer messages should be transmitted on a working channel.

If the message is addressed to 'all stations' and is primarily intended for reception by other vessels in the vicinity, then VHF will be used both for the DSC alert and the subsequent traffic and the message itself could be transmitted on channel 6, the inter-ship safety channel, or channel 13, the bridge-to-bridge navigational safety channel. For example, if you were entering a narrow channel in thick fog and you wanted to warn other vessels of your location, you would do this on channel 13.

Transmission of a Safety Alert

As with the urgency call, DSC is used to alert a station or stations that there is a safety message about to be transmitted and advises them of the frequency and mode. To send a DSC safety alert:

a. Tune the radio to the DSC frequency of the band on which it is desired to transmit the alert.
b. Select 'safety call' on the DSC control unit.
c. Address the call to 'all stations' or to the MMSI of a particular Coast Station or vessel or group of vessels.

d. Key in the channel on which the urgency message will be transmitted. For most safety messages a working channel (such as VHF channel 13 or 6) is selected, rather than the emergency channel.
e. Transmit the DSC safety alert.

Transmission of a Safety Message

The radio can now be tuned to the appropriate channel and the message transmitted. The message should be in the format:

Securité – The word *securité* – pronounced securitay – indicates that this is a safety message.

Address – The message must be addressed to somebody, very often in this case to 'all stations'.

Identity – Give your MMSI, which will have been given in the DSC call, and the name of your vessel and/or call-sign. All transmissions must be identified, even if you are not expecting a reply.

Message – The text of the safety message.

Out – Terminate the transmission with the name/call-sign of the vessel, and the word 'out', which signifies the end of the transmission and that you are not expecting a reply. 'over' signifies the end of that part of the transmission and that you are standing by for a reply. Although one hears it every day, it is incorrect to say 'over and out' – the two together are contradictory.

Reception of a Safety Alert

Another vessel may want to issue a safety message to warn of a danger to navigation, or perhaps a Coast Station has an urgent gale warning or navigational warning to transmit. The DSC alert may be addressed to 'All Stations', a group of vessels, vessels in a particular area, or it may be addressed to you specifically. If the DSC control unit recognises that the safety call concerns you, you will be alerted.

a. Do not acknowledge by DSC, unless the alert is addressed only to your vessel.
b. Tune the radio to the frequency and mode indicated in the call
c. Listen for the transmitted message.

Non-DSC equipped vessels should make distress, urgency, or safety calls on the emergency frequency of a suitable band prior to transmitting the message. The call is Mayday, repeated three times, for a distress call; Pan Pan repeated three times for an urgency call; or *Securité* repeated three times for a safety call. This should be followed by your vessel's name and/or call sign again repeated three times. Then the message should be transmitted in exactly the same way as if a DSC alert had been sent, e.g., MIPDANIO for distress.

Under the GMDSS regulations there is no obligation for anybody to monitor any of the emergency frequencies other than the DSC frequencies, although hopefully somebody will hear you.

Routine Calls on VHF

Routine calls cover all non-emergency traffic. From your vessel you may wish to call shore stations or other vessels, or you might receive calls from shore or from other vessels.

Transmission of Routine VHF Calls to Coast Stations

Coast Stations are commercial radio stations that exist to make telephone connections between ships at sea and telephone subscribers ashore.

On VHF, channel 70 is used with DSC not only for distress, urgency and safety calls but it is used for routine calls as well. DSC is used to alert the called station and to agree a working channel. The communication is then carried out on that working channel.

a. Tune the radio to VHF channel 70.
b. Key in MMSI of the Coast Station
c. Select category of call – Routine.
d. Do not select a working channel – the Coast Station will do that.
e. Transmit the DSC call.

The Coast Station will send a DSC acknowledgement and part of that acknowledgement will include the working channel that they wish to use. Tune the VHF radio to that channel, listen to make sure that there is not other traffic in progress, and begin the call:

MMSI or name of Coast Station

This is....... Your MMSI, and the name and call-sign of your vessel.

State what traffic you have.

The Coast Station will ask for the telephone number that you want and how the call is to be paid (see Chapter 19). Then they will ask you to stand by while they connect you. Normally the Coast Station transmits a series of pips while you are standing by. This to let other vessels know that the channel is occupied and they should not try calling on that channel.

When the Coast Station has your party on the line, they will tell you to go ahead. Remember that unless you have a duplex radio, only one of you can talk at a time, so it will probably help to say 'over' at the end of each transmission to let the other person know that they can talk.

If the Coast Station does not acknowledge your DSC call, then you should wait five minutes before repeating the call. If there is still no DSC acknowledgement received, then you must wait a further 15 minutes before trying again.

Vessels that are not DSC-equipped will probably be able to continue to call the Coast Stations on their working channels for the foreseeable future. Many Coast Stations, and certainly all those in the UK, can detect a transmission on any of their VHF working channels. To call them, it is only necessary to key the microphone for a few seconds. The station will automatically begin to transmit the 'pips' on that channel to indicate to you that your call has been received and to others that the channel is occupied. As soon as an operator is available they will ask, on that channel, who is calling them. That is your invitation to reply, giving the name of your vessel, the call-sign, and what traffic you have for them.

If keying the microphone does not automatically initiate the pips being transmitted, then call the Coast Station by name on the working channel, and they should respond to you. Some Coast Stations may elect to continue to monitor channel 16. This information will be available in the appropriate list of radio signals.

When making a call direct on a working channel, it is essential that you listen for a few minutes to make sure that there is nobody already using the channel, and that there are no pips being transmitted. Only call if the working channel is silent and obviously not being used.

It is possible to make automatic telephone calls on VHF through some Coast Stations without any intervention on the part of an operator. Some DSC control units have the facility for including the telephone number in the DSC call, but to make fully automatic calls, a special dialling unit is required. The normal procedure is to call the Coast Station directly on a working channel. The telephone number that you require, and the PIN for your account, are transmitted to the Coast Station by the dialling unit. A computer records your PIN for charging purposes, and automatically connects the call to the requested number.

Other shore stations that you might want to contact could include Port Control, Pilot Stations or the office in a marina. Some of these may be slow to embrace the DSC technology and may have to be called by voice direct on their working channel. Vessels not equipped with DSC will have to try and call them direct on their working channel or possibly on channel 16. As before, listen to the channel first to make sure that it is clear then call the station by name and give your vessel's name and call-sign.

The working channel for a particular station can be found in the appropriate list of radio signals or the Almanac for that area.

Transmission of Routine VHF Calls to Other Vessels
This procedure is similar to calling a Coast Station, except this time *you* suggest a working channel. As we said before, theoretically under GMDSS all initial calls are supposed to be made by DSC. If you are trying to call a DSC-equipped vessel, and you know their **M**aritime **M**obile **S**ervice **I**dentity number then it is simple, all you do is send them a DSC call addressed to their MMSI number indicating a suggested working channel – one of the recognised inter-ship working channels, such as 8 or 72.

It is good practice to listen to the working channel that you are proposing, before sending the DSC call so that you do not suggest switching to one that is already occupied.

a. Tune the radio to VHF channel 70.
b. Key in MMSI of the other vessel.
c. Select category of call – routine.
d. Key in the proposed working channel.
e. Transmit the DSC call.

The called vessel, if he is free to handle the traffic, will send a DSC Acknowledgement, at which point you switch to the channel you chose and call them on voice. The correct way to call is to put their name first:

Name of vessel that you are calling – There should be no need to call them three times, as the initial contact has already been made by DSC

This is......... – (name and call sign of your vessel).

Over – This is their invitation to transmit.

It is always the 'called vessel' who controls the traffic. If he is unable to handle the traffic at that moment, then it is up to him to call back to the calling station when he is able to accept the traffic.

If you are trying to call an unknown vessel, perhaps a vessel you can see on a collision course, the only way to do this by DSC is to call 'all stations'. To save getting responses from vessels miles away, you can either transmit the DSC call on low power, if the DSC control unit will allow it, or address the call to all stations in a particular area and make that area a circular zone within say five miles of your position. Only vessels within that zone should receive the call.

If the call is to discuss a possible collision situation, then you are more likely to get the attention of the other vessel by making the call a 'safety call'.

The frequency you should nominate in your DSC call in this situation would be channel 13.

It is likely that most commercial ships will continue to monitor channel 13, particularly when in confined waters, for direct bridge-to-bridge communications as well as the obligatory DSC channel 70. So a call direct on channel 13, by voice is likely to succeed without using the DSC at all.

A non-DSC equipped vessel, especially when navigating in confined waters, should be able to contact an approaching ship by calling them directly on channel 13. To call other vessels, a non-DSC equipped vessel should try calling on channel 16, but there is no obligation under GMDSS for anybody to monitor channel 16.

Reception of Routine Calls on VHF
If you receive a DSC call from another vessel or from a Coast Station and you are in a position to be able to talk to them, acknowledge by DSC and switch to the indicated channel and listen for their call:

a. Tune the VHF radio to channel 70
b. Select 'acknowledge' on the DSC control unit.
c. Confirm that the proposed working channel is suitable and transmit the acknowledgement.
d. Tune the radio to the proposed channel and listen for their call.

A non-DSC equipped vessel should monitor channel 16, and if possible, channel 13 as well to receive calls.

Routine Calls on MF
Transmission of Routine MF Calls to Coast Stations
Once again, the initial contact should be by DSC. Routine calls should not be made on the emergency frequency. There is a national DSC calling frequency nominated by each country and in most cases an individual Coast Station will have its own DSC calling frequency. This information is available from the appropriate list of radio signals.

If the DSC frequency of the Coast Station is not known, then use the International DSC MF calling frequency which can normally be used between ships and Coast Stations of different nationality. This is a duplex frequency, so the vessel transmits on one frequency and then listens for the Coast Station to reply on another frequency. For DSC calling, the ship transmits on 2189.5 kHz and listens on 2177 kHz. The procedure to make a call to a Coast Station is:

a. Tune the MF radio to transmit on the required DSC frequency. If the particular frequency is unknown, then use 2189.5 kHz. The MF receiver on your DSC control unit should be scanning various frequencies for a reply – as a minimum it should scan 2177 kHz and 2187.5 kHz
b. Key in the MMSI of the Coast Station
c. Select category of call – routine.
d. Select mode for traffic – voice or telex
e. Do not select a working channel – the Coast Station will do that.
f. Transmit the DSC call.

The Coast Station will send a DSC acknowledgement and part of that acknowledgement will include the working channel. Tune the MF radio to that channel, which will almost certainly be a duplex channel, with one frequency for transmit and another for receive. Respond on the working channel by voice or telex with:

MMSI or name of Coast Station

This is....... Your MMSI, and the name and call-sign of your vessel.

State what traffic you have.

If you are calling the Coast Station on telex, remember to set the mode on the radio to J2B, but since you are in contact with just one station use ARQ rather than using FEC as we did for the distress, urgency and safety messages. If the traffic is to be on voice, then select J3E for the mode.

Transmission of Routine MF Calls to Other Vessels
Routine DSC calls to other vessels should not be made on the DSC emergency frequency, but on the DSC international calling frequency of 2177 kHz. DSC calls between vessels use 2177 kHz as a simplex frequency rather than as one of a duplex pair as when calling a Coast Station.

a. Tune the MF radio to transmit on the DSC calling frequency of 2177 kHz
b. Key in MMSI of the vessel you wish to call
c. Select category of call – routine.
d. Select mode for traffic – voice or telex
e. Select a working frequency. It is best to listen to the proposed frequency before sending the call so that you do not choose one that is already occupied.
f. Transmit the DSC call.

The called vessel, if he is in a position to be able to respond, will send a DSC acknowledgement. Tune the radio to the nominated frequency and mode and call the other vessel by voice or telex:

MMSI and name of other vessel.
This is....... (Your MMSI, and the name and call-sign of your vessel.) It is important to include your MMSI because that is the only part of your identity which was included in your DSC call.
Over.

Wait for a response from the other vessel, then continue with your communication.

Reception of Routine MF Calls

As a minimum, the MF receiver on the DSC control unit should be monitoring the emergency DSC frequency of 2187.5 kHz and the international calling frequency of 2177 kHz. It may also be able to scan other specified DSC frequencies which are used by particular Coast Stations, or organisations.

When the DSC control unit indicates that there is a call for your vessel:

a. Tune the MF radio to the required DSC frequency for the acknowledgement. If the call is from another vessel, the frequency will be 2177 kHz. If from a Coast Station it will be 2189.5 kHz, or another designated frequency.
b. Select the acknowledge format on the DSC control unit.
c. The calling station should have indicated a proposed working frequency and mode in his DSC call. If this is acceptable, transmit your DSC acknowledgement.
d. Tune the MF transmitter and receiver to the indicated mode and frequencies, and listen for the call.
e. Answer the call with your vessel's MMSI and the name and call-sign.

A non-DSC equipped vessel should monitor 2182 kHz for any calls on MF. If it is expecting traffic through a particular Coast Station, then the operator should listen to the traffic list that the Coast Station will broadcast on one of its working frequencies at scheduled times.

Routine calls on HF

Transmission of Routine HF Calls to a Coast Station

The procedure for making routine DSC calls to a Coast Station on HF is similar to that used on MF. The emergency frequencies are not used for routine calls. The most appropriate band for the anticipated propagation conditions is chosen and the Coast Station is called either on the national DSC frequency for that band or the station's own DSC frequency. The calling vessel should indicate the preferred mode of working (voice or telex) but should not suggest a working frequency. The Coast Station will do that in their DSC acknowledgement.

a. Tune the radio to the appropriate DSC calling frequency.
b. Key in the MMSI of the station you are calling
c. Select 'routine.'
d. Do not select a working frequency for the traffic, the Coast Station will do that. You should indicate if the traffic is to be on voice or telex.
e. Transmit the DSC call, and wait for an acknowledgement. Two consecutive calls may be transmitted on the same frequency with a pause of 45 seconds between them. This allows a scanning receiver time to hear the call.

When the DSC acknowledgement is received, tune the HF radio to the indicated frequency, and prepare to send the traffic. If the communication is to be by voice, the correct mode is J3E. If it is going to be transmitted on telex, then select J2B, and since you are transmitting to just one station, use ARQ.

If no DSC acknowledgement in received from the Coast Station, you are supposed to wait for thirty minutes before repeating the DSC call. Alternatively, if no reply is received within five minutes, then you can try transmitting the DSC call on another band. Try a higher band in daylight or a lower one at night and repeat the procedure until an acknowledgement is received.

Once contact is established on a working frequency with the Coast Station, if the communication is by voice, then at many Coast Stations a technical operator will usually spend a few moments making adjustments, or changing antennas, to improve the signal as much as possible. When he is satisfied with the signal he will hand you over to the telephone operator. When you have finished with all your traffic, you should wait for the telephone operator to hand you back to the technical operator before signing off.

DSC would not normally be used to establish calls on HF between vessels. Normally a time and frequency would be agreed ahead of time and the vessels would simply call each other 'on schedule' on one of the inter-ship simplex frequencies.

Reception of Routine Calls on HF
If the receiver in the DSC control unit can be programmed to scan HF frequencies other than the just the HF emergency frequencies, then it should be possible to monitor the DSC calling channels of one or more Coast Stations. If the Coast Station receives a call for you and they know your MMSI then it will be possible for them to call you by DSC. If you cannot monitor their frequencies or if the caller does not know your MMSI, then you will have to listen to the traffic lists broadcast by the Coast Stations.

Non-DSC equipped vessels will have to continue to call Coast Stations on their working frequencies to place calls and listen to the scheduled traffic lists to receive calls on the HF bands.

71

DSC Testing Procedures.

VHF

For the VHF DSC there are no special provisions for testing. The correct operation can be verified by making a routine DSC call on channel 70, preferably to another vessel, but failing that to a Coast Station. DSC test calls, as such, are not permitted on channel 70.

MF

On MF, test calls can be made, and indeed, for compulsory vessels they must be made on a weekly basis. The use of the emergency frequency 2187.5 kHz should be avoided as far as possible. An individual Coast Station should be called, preferably on the national calling frequency, but if that is not known then the international calling frequency can be used – the ship transmits on 2189.5 kHz and listens on 2177 kHz. The procedure is as follows:

a. Tune the radio to the appropriate MF DSC transmit frequency – the receiver in the DSC control unit should be monitoring the receive frequency.
b. Select the 'test call' mode on the DSC control unit.
c. Key in the MMSI of the chosen Coast Station.
d. Check as far as possible that there are no other calls in progress, and transmit the DSC test call.
e. The Coast Station should acknowledge by DSC, and no further communication is needed. If no acknowledgement is received, you must wait five minutes before trying again. If that call also fails to be acknowledged, then you must wait a further 15 minutes before making another attempt.

HF

Test calls can be made on HF, and again as far as possible, the use of the DSC Emergency frequencies should be avoided. A test call should be made to an individual Coast Station, taking into account likely propagation conditions, using the same procedure as for MF.

CHAPTER 8

On Scene Distress Communications

Control of Distress Communications

In a distress situation, normally there will be a Coast Station or a Rescue Co-ordination Centre running the operation. They will have the overall responsibility for organising other vessels and/or aircraft to help in the search and rescue.

If there are a number of vessels involved in the rescue, an On Scene Commander will be appointed from amongst those vessels or aircraft. The OSC or the RCC will choose what frequency will be used for the distress communications. The communications will be in simplex, and one of the simplex distress frequencies will most likely be used:

channel 16 VHF, 2182 kHz voice, or 2174.5 kHz telex on MF.

Telex will be slower than voice for communications but it has the advantage that there is a written record available of the communications. If telex is used, then FEC mode should be selected so that all stations can copy the traffic.

If aircraft are involved in the search, it is possible that they may be able to communicate on VHF channel 16 and/or on 2182 kHz, especially if they are dedicated Search And Rescue aircraft. If they do not have these frequencies, then it should be possible to communicate with them on 3023 kHz, 4125 kHz, or 5680 kHz on HF voice.

Once the situation is reasonably under control, the OSC or the RCC may elect to move VHF traffic off channel 16. They could choose channel 06, the Primary Inter-ship safety channel. If the UK Coast Guard are involved, then they will probably move the traffic to channel 67, and the US Coast Guard will use 22A.

While the traffic is still on a distress frequency, the controlling station, i.e. the Coast Station, the RCC, or the OSC can impose radio silence on any other stations that might be interfering with the distress working. On voice, they will make the announcement SEELONCE MAYDAY, or if the traffic is on telex, SILENCE MAYDAY. On hearing this announcement, all stations not directly concerned in the distress situation are forbidden to transmit on that frequency until the controlling station gives them permission to do so.

As the situation comes under control, the RCC or the OSC may transmit the signal PRUDONCE. This signifies that there is still distress working on the frequency, but total radio silence is no longer required. Other stations may use the frequency for urgent traffic, but should be careful not to interfere with any of the distress traffic.

Any vessel, or indeed aircraft, which is involved in the distress situation and is suffering from interference from another station on the frequency, can call SEELONCE DISTRESS. Other vessels hearing this should avoid transmitting on the frequency until given leave to do so. Note that it is only the OSC or the RCC who should call SEELONCE MAYDAY, for anybody else it is SEELONCE DISTRESS.

When the situation has been resolved, or the distress traffic is being transferred to another frequency, the OSC or the RCC will lift the silence restrictions with a call saying SEELONCE FEENEE, or on telex, SILENCE FINI. Other stations are now free to use the frequency.

CHAPTER 9

Satellite
Communications

An Overall View

The Inmarsat satellite system is concerned with two kinds of communication as far as maritime stations are concerned – the transmission of emergency traffic, such as distress, urgency and safety messages, to and from vessels at sea, and for routine communications, also in both directions.

The Inmarsat system of global satellite communication was proposed by the International Maritime Organisation as a way of overcoming congestion and atmospheric interference. The developing satellite technology of the 1970s made it become a reality and the system became commercially operational in 1982.

When Inmarsat first started operations it leased capacity on existing satellites. Its initial operations were exclusively concerned with maritime stations, but the system soon expanded as aeronautical and land users realised the benefits of the system and Inmarsat began to launch its own satellites. At the present time, maritime stations still generate about two thirds of the system's traffic.

The world according to Inmarsat is divided into four regions:

Atlantic Ocean Region East.   Atlantic Ocean Region West
Indian Ocean Region   Pacific Ocean Region

There is a satellite, and usually at least one spare, in geostationary orbit at a height of about 36,000 km over each region. The present (1997) orbital locations of the satellites are:

Ocean Region	Main Satellite	Location	Spare Satellite	Location
AOR-E	Inmarsat-2 F2	15.5 degs W	Marecs – B2	15 degs W
AOR-W	Inmarsat-2 F4	54 degs W	Inmarsat-2 F2	31 degs W
IOR	Inmarsat-3 F1	64 degs E	Inmarsat-2 F3	65 degs E
POR	Inmarsat-2 F3	178 degs E	Marisat-F3	182 degs E

Each satellite can 'see' about one third of the Earth, so there is some overlap between adjacent regions. From a **M**obile **E**arth **S**tation, in our case the vessel wishing to communicate, the satellite being used must be at an elevation of at least 5 degrees above the horizon for there to be reliable communications. Since the four satellites are in orbit over the equator, this means that the very high latitudes of the polar regions cannot be covered. The area of coverage is effectively from about 70° N to about 70° S.

On the ground there are 34 **L**and **E**arth **S**tations, which provide the link between the satellites and the terrestrial telecommunications network. Not all of the LESs can provide all the services so a suitable LES, which is within the footprint of the satellite being worked, must be chosen. The LESs are sometimes called **C**oast **E**arth **S**tations and they are the satellite equivalent of the HF or VHF Coast Stations. However, since there is no necessity for a satellite earth station to be on the coast, and since one third of the mobile traffic generated on the satellite system is from non-maritime mobile stations, **L**and **E**arth **S**tation is probably the better term to use.

Each LES is assigned a two-digit code number. If that LES can access more than one satellite, then the same code number is used through each satellite that the LES can access. Some LESs in Europe can actually access three satellites, the only one beyond their reach is the Pacific Ocean Region. For any satellite that the LES cannot access, that particular code number could well be allocated to another LES on that satellite.

For example, 01 through AOR-W, or through AOR-E is Southbury LES in the eastern USA, but 01 through the POR is Santa Paula on the west coast of the USA. 02 via AOR-W is Goonhilly in the UK, but on the POR or IOR satellite it is Perth in Australia. So care must be taken that the antenna is pointing at the correct satellite, or in the case of Inmarsat C, that you are logged onto the correct satellite before the code for the LES is entered.

In each Ocean Region there is a **N**etwork **C**o-ordination **S**tation. Each NCS continuously monitors the flow of traffic through its satellite and ensures that calls are set up correctly. The NCS is permanently connected to all the LESs that are working through that particular satellite, and it monitors them all to ensure that they are functioning correctly. The NCS allocates the channel to be used by the mobile station and by the LES for each and every call. All the NCSs are in turn monitored and controlled by the Network Control Centre. The NCC is at the Inmarsat Headquarters in London and it is permanently connected to all the NCSs.

Finally, there is the Satellite Control Centre, also located in London, which is responsible for looking after the satellites themselves. The SCC is linked to a series of tracking stations around the world and it monitors the orbit of each satellite, adjusting it as necessary to keep the satellite exactly where it is supposed to be.

In 1990, Inmarsat launched the first of its own second-generation satellites and by April 1992, each region had a Series 2 satellite. These satellites were built by a consortium headed by the Space and Communications Division of British Aerospace. The Series 2 satellites were designed with an expected ten-year life. Each weighed some 1,300 kilos at launch and has 1,200 watts of available power – more than twice the power of the original satellites.

These satellites in turn are being replaced by Series 3 satellites – the first of which was launched in 1996, and by now, the fourth and last should be in position. These are a lot more powerful again – eight times the power of the Series 2, and some twenty times as powerful as the originals. In addition to the global beam, each of these new satellites has five spot-beams. These are focused onto specific areas of the earth, just as a searchlight might be. This not only focuses the energy into smaller areas, so allowing operation at much lower energy levels, but it also allows the same frequency to be used at the same time in different areas but through the same satellite. This increases the scope for greater numbers of calls to be carried at any given moment. This spot-beam technology, with its lower energy requirement, has opened the door to the possibility of a global portable phone system.

The newer satellites can also support a special type of EPIRB called the Inmarsat E type. We will look at these in detail in the section devoted to EPIRBs.

With the EPIRB service there are now six Inmarsat services which may be of interest to the mariner. Each service has its own merits and disadvantages. For compulsory GMDSS vessels, not all of the systems can be GMDSS certified. Let's look at each system in turn.

Inmarsat A

This is the old original Analogue system, which began operation in 1982. Although A is now classed as rather old technology, new stations are still joining the system, and there are now some 22,000 mobile stations of various sorts operating Inmarsat A.

Inmarsat A can support two-way telephone, telex, fax, E-mail and with the **High Speed Data** option, it can support data transmission up to 64 kilobits per second. In addition to supporting simultaneous two-way data transmission, the HSD option can be used for the transmission of still pictures and compressed video pictures or for video conference calls.

Inmarsat A can support **Enhanced Group Calling** – the reception of **Maritime Safety Information** which can be sent to 'All Stations', or to a group of vessels, or to vessels in a specific region. The ability to receive EGC is a pre-requisite for GMDSS certification. Some Inmarsat A terminals will require the fitting of an external EGC receiver for reception of these MSIs.

The mobile station communicates with the satellite on frequencies in the L-band – 1.5 to 1.6 GHz (remember, that is 1,600 MHz, or 1,600,000 kHz). The satellite in turn communicates with the LES on frequencies in the C- band – 4 to 6 GHz.

There are two principle drawbacks to the Inmarsat A system – it is the most expensive of all of them in terms of call charges, and because it uses high bandwidth and relatively low power, it needs a large parabolic antenna. On board a vessel at sea, this antenna must be kept constantly pointed at the satellite regardless of how the vessel moves. This requires gyroscopes, motors and considerable power. A typical marine Inmarsat A antenna is housed in a dome up to one and a half metres in diameter, and weighs around a hundred kilos. Certainly not something suitable for a small yacht.

Inmarsat B

Inmarsat B is the newer digital version of the analogue Inmarsat A. (A for **A**nalogue and B for **B**inary!) The digital technology makes better use of the bandwidth and the satellite power which results in lower call charges, although the initial equipment cost is higher than for A.

It is possible for larger vessels to be fitted with an extra large, high-gain antenna. This can operate with much lower satellite power and so call charges using this system are about half the normal B charges. However, even the normal B antenna is large, virtually identical to the dome of an A system, so the extra large antenna can really only be fitted to big commercial ships where space and weight are not a consideration.

Inmarsat B supports direct-dial telephone, fax and telex calls, and with the **High Speed Data** link, simultaneous two-way high speed data can be transferred, including pictures and video.

It is the intention for Inmarsat B to supersede A, but it is likely that both systems will coexist for a number of years. At the present time B does not support **E**nhanced **G**roup **C**alling for the reception of **M**aritime **S**afety **I**nformation, and so it cannot be GMDSS approved for compulsory vessels. A compulsory GMDSS vessel equipped with Inmarsat B could either fit a stand-alone EGC receiver or an Inmarsat C system for reception of the MSIs.

Inmarsat C

Inmarsat C supports only data transmission, not voice. It does allow **E**nhanced **G**roup **C**alling, and it is the system of choice for compliance with the GMDSS. Data is transferred at a rate of 600 bits/second and call charges are based on the number of bits of data transferred. Inmarsat C terminals are suitable for almost any size of vessel. The power requirement is minimal, the unit itself is normally a small 'black box' which is interfaced with a computer, and best of all, the antenna is a very small fixed antenna – there are no big and power hungry gyros, just a little, plastic, fixed antenna, similar to that used by GPS navigation receivers.

There are several different services which Inmarsat C offers:

Two way messaging

The normal method of communication on Inmarsat C is by store-and-forward telex. Messages up to 32 kilobytes – probably about 6,000 words, can be sent in either direction. Messages from the mobile station are transmitted via the satellite to an appropriate **L**and **E**arth **S**tation – there are 25 LESs at the present time (1997) which can handle Inmarsat C traffic, but that number is increasing almost daily. The data is sent in packets to the LES where it is reassembled into the complete message. The message is then sent to the addressee by the national or international telecommunications network. It can be delivered to a fax, telex or E-mail address, or failing any of these, the message can be printed and be sent by mail. Messages sent in the reverse direction can be sent to an individual vessel, or simultaneously to a group of vessels.

Polling and data reporting

Polling allows a shore station to interrogate a mobile station at any time. Such polling will trigger the automatic transmission of the required pre-programmed information. Such information could be the position of the vessel, its course and speed, or the read-out of any on-board sensors.

Data reporting allows for the automatic transmission of short packets of information at fixed pre-arranged intervals.

Position reporting

An Inmarsat C terminal can easily be interfaced with a wide variety of navigation systems such as Decca, Loran or GPS. The derived position can be transmitted automatically at fixed intervals or on demand.

Distress alerting

Marine Inmarsat C terminals are equipped with a special facility, which when activated, automatically generates and transmits a priority distress message to the **R**escue **C**o-ordination **C**entre. If the terminal is linked to a navigational system, the message will automatically include the position of the vessel.

Enhanced Group Calling

This is the feature of Inmarsat C which makes it so valuable to the GMDSS. Using EGC, messages can be sent to groups of vessels, via SafetyNET or FleetNET.

SafetyNET provides an efficient and low cost method of sending **M**aritime **S**afety **I**nformation to vessels at sea. The messages can be restricted to individual vessels, or to vessels in a particular geographic area. This service is used by meteorological and hydrographic authorities for issuing forecasts or warnings, as well as by Coast Guard and Search and Rescue centres for disseminating MSIs, and for co-ordinating rescue in a distress situation.

FleetNET is a commercial service which allows the sending of messages to a virtually unlimited number of terminals simultaneously. This could be all the vessels in a particular race, or perhaps all the vessels belonging to one company. It could even be everybody who subscribes to a particular service, such as stock exchange reports or specialised weather analyses.

Inmarsat E

E is the **E**mergency system within Inmarsat. There are three LESs which are equipped to receive Inmarsat E signals, from the four Ocean Regions. These stations are at:

Niles Canyon, USA – **A**tlantic **O**cean **R**egion – **W**est
Perth, Australia   – **I**ndian **O**cean **R**egion
Raisting, Germany – **A**tlantic **O**cean **R**egion – **E**ast
Niles Canyon and Perth share responsibility for **P**acific **O**cean **R**egion.

When an Inmarsat E EPIRB transmits a distress message to one of the satellites the message is instantly relayed to the LES, from where it is sent to the appropriate Rescue Co-ordination Centre who can then organise and co-ordinate the rescue.

The biggest advantage of this type of EPIRB is that since the satellites are geostationary they are always in view, so there is no waiting for a satellite to appear over the horizon. This means that distress messages are relayed almost instantaneously. The disadvantage is that since the satellites are geo-stationary, they cannot determine where the casualty is. The EPIRB itself must be combined with a GPS navigation receiver so that the position can be included as part of the message. This contributes not only to the bulk of the equipment but also to the cost. We will take a look at the various types of EPIRBs in a later section.

Inmarsat M

The 'M' is for Mobile, not marine. By far the greatest number of M units are land mobile units. M does not support Enhanced Group Calling, so it is not approved for compulsory equipment for GMDSS compliance. However, marine M units usually incorporate a distress-alerting button and so are suitable for use at sea on non-compulsory GMDSS vessels, although MSIs will not be received.

As Inmarsat M is a digital system, it uses minimal bandwidth and power, resulting in lower call charges than A. M offers good quality two-way voice communications, slow speed facsimile, and slow speed data (2.4 kbit/sec) transmission and reception.

The equipment costs and call charges are higher than C, but M does allow voice traffic. At sea, a steerable parabolic antenna is required. This is similar in operation to the antenna used for A and B, but it is very much smaller, lighter and cheaper.

Inmarsat Phone Mini-M

Phone Mini-M is the result of the new spot-beam technology. Each of the series 3 satellites has five spot-beams, focused on areas of greatest use. These beams focus not only the energy being transmitted from the satellite, but also allow the very weak signals from the mobile stations to be received. This allows the use of truly portable telephones within the satellite system. The mini-M phones are not unlike the ubiquitous cell-phones, but unlike the cell-phones, they offer close to global communications. The current units are about the size and weight of a laptop computer and use a flat-plate antenna.

The mini-M can support two-way voice, fax and data transmission. The principal advantage is the extreme portability of the units. The disadvantage, as far as we are concerned, is that it does not support Enhanced Group Calling, and so cannot be GMDSS approved and since the beams are focused on areas of high traffic, considerable areas of the world's oceans are outside the beams. In these areas, the mini-M system cannot be used at all. Also, the flat-plate antenna has to be pointed in the general direction of the satellite and on board a small vessel in a big sea, this is not always easy to achieve.

Next we will take a look at the specific operation of Inmarsat A and C, which as we have already seen, are the only two satellite communication systems which can be GMDSS approved for compulsory vessels.

Operation of GMDSS Approved Satellite Communication Systems

The description of the operation of satellite systems must obviously be kept in general terms as much of the physical operation of the equipment depends on the equipment itself. However, there are some basic principles involved and some standard protocols to be observed. More detailed information can be obtained from the manufacturer's handbook and the operator should become thoroughly familiar with the equipment. We will restrict ourselves to the marine applications of the systems.

Inmarsat A

The operation of A is essentially similar to B, it is really only the technology and the way that the signal is actually transmitted that is different. A uses an Analogue signal, and B is Digital. We will look at the operation of A in detail, remembering that B is virtually the same.

The basic services offered by A are:

- distress communication
- automatic dialling for telephone calls, telex and facsimile, to and from the vessel.

Other services which may not be available through all the LESs include:

- the transmission of medium speed or high speed data.
- group calling – where several mobile stations can be called at the same time, by voice or data
- medical assistance
- maritime assistance
- technical assistance
- other telephone facilities such as collect calls, credit card calls, person-to-person, telephone enquiries etc.

Before communications can begin, with any system using a steerable antenna the antenna must be pointed at the satellite. Because of the overlap of the global beams of the satellites, often the vessel can be in the footprint of two, or even three, of the four satellites, so the first job is to decide which satellite to use. Charges are levied not only on satellite time but also for the use of the ground telecommunications network, so it is generally cheaper to use the LES which is closest to the eventual addressee. If the vessel is in a region where there is a choice of satellites, choose the one which will give access to the LES which is closest to the final destination of the call.

The elevation (height) of the satellite and its azimuth (bearing) from the vessel's location must be found. There are two ways to do this. For each satellite a chart is issued, which covers the footprint of the satellite. If the vessel's position is marked on the chart, then the elevation and azimuth of the satellite can be read directly off the chart.

The other method is to use tables which are common to all four satellites. There are four of these tables, one for each quadrant that the vessel could be in, in relation to the satellite. The vessel can be north and east, north and west, south and east, or south and west of the satellite. From the ship's position, determine which of the tables to use. The tables are entered using the ship's latitude (to the nearest five degrees), and the difference in longitude between the ship and the satellite, that is, how far east or west of the satellite the ship is. The elevation and azimuth can be read from the table.

The elevation and azimuth are entered into the terminal and the antenna moves to that position to search for the signal from the satellite. Once the antenna has found the satellite it should remain locked on to it regardless of the movement of the vessel. The control unit continuously moves the antenna by small amounts, always seeking the strongest signal. Provided the equipment is left running, no further adjustment to the antenna should be necessary unless the vessel moves into another ocean region, or if the vessel is in an area served by two satellites and it is desired to use an LES which is only available through the other satellite. In either of these cases, the set-up routine must be completed again and the antenna locked onto the other satellite.

A vessel which is likely to change Ocean Regions, and therefore change satellites, should always include in any messages the identification of the satellite they will be monitoring if they are expecting to receive any calls from shore. Otherwise it may not be possible for the incoming traffic to be routed to the correct satellite.

Depending on the location of the antenna on board the vessel, there may be certain directions in which the antenna is shielded from the satellite by structures on board the vessel, especially when the satellite is at low elevations. The operator should be aware of any such limitations and care should be taken not to alter course while communications are in progress, as this could put the satellite into a blind sector of the antenna.

A large blind sector could cause the antenna to lose the satellite which would result in having to run the set-up procedure again. If a new antenna is being installed, great care should be taken to try to eliminate any blind spots or at least reduce them to an acceptable minimum. The antenna should also be mounted in such a way that nobody can be close to it when the set is transmitting. A beam of microwaves pointed straight at a person's head can be very dangerous.

Once the antenna is locked on to the selected satellite, it is normal to leave the equipment running so that the set is always available for communication, be it the routine sending or receiving of messages or a distress situation.

Transmission of Distress Calls on Inmarsat A

Operators of any Inmarsat equipment must familiarise themselves with the operation of the distress facilities of the specific equipment which is bound to vary between manufacturers. A look at the principles involved follows.

The ITU recommends that distress traffic is done by telex rather than by voice. This gives a written record of all traffic, and reduces the chance for confusion. However, if time is short it may be better to use voice.

To initiate a distress call, assuming the antenna is locked onto a satellite:

1. Select mode – voice or telex.
2. Select distress priority – Priority 3.
3. Select an LES, and key in the number for the appropriate **R**escue **C**o-ordination **C**entre if necessary. Some LESs will automatically route a distress Priority 3 call to the nearest RCC, others will require the number of the RCC to be dialled, while for the remainder, a Priority 3 call will automatically bring operator assistance. If for some reason the call does not go through, then the **N**etwork **C**o-ordination **S**tation should recognise the call as Priority 3, and either route it directly to the RCC, or an operator will interrupt the call and assist.
4. Once connected to the RCC then the distress message should be sent. It is important to follow the recommended format for a distress message, so that all the information is given in the order of importance, in case subsequent communication is lost.

As always, the distress message should be composed using the mnemonic MIPDANIO.

Mayday – Start the message with the word Mayday, or SOS on telex.

Identity – This is……….. (call-sign and name of vessel).

84

Position – Either as latitude and longitude, or distance and bearing *from* a conspicuous landmark.

Distress – The nature of the distress, e.g. sinking, explosion, pirate attack etc.

Assistance – Assistance needed, e.g. help to abandon ship, put out a fire etc.

Numbers of persons involved – The rescuers will then know how many people to look for.

Information – Any other information that might be useful to the rescuers, such as wind and sea conditions.

Over.

Priority 3 calls must only be made in a distress situation – when the vessel or a person is in grave *and* imminent danger. All other calls, including urgency and safety calls are to be made as Priority 0. The appropriate service code is then used to differentiate urgent and routine calls. The more important service codes are:

00	Automatic service	Used for making direct dial calls, using the International Direct Dial codes.
11	International Operator	Information from the International Operator in the country where the LES is situated
12	International Information	Information about subscribers in countries other than where the LES is situated
13	National Operator	Assistance in making calls within the country where the LES is situated
14	National Information	Information about subscribers in the country where the LES is situated
31	Maritime Enquiries	Information regarding ship location or authorisation
32	Medical Advice	The LES will connect you with a hospital or doctor, to get medical *advice*. Use 38 for assistance.
33	Technical Assistance	Technical staff at the LES should normally be available to offer assistance with equipment problems.
34	Person-to-Person Calls	Calls are made via the operator.
35	Collect Calls	Calls are made via the operator.
36	Credit Card Calls	Calls are made via the operator and charged to a charge card or credit card.
37	Time and Charges	Received either as a call back from the operator or as a short telex message.

38	Medical *Assistance*	Used for *urgent* medical assistance, such as medical evacuation or for a doctor to board the vessel. This is equivalent to a 'Pan Pan Medico' call. Use 32 for medical advice.
39	Maritime *Assistance*	Used for urgent assistance, such as needing a tow. Equivalent to a Pan Pan call. Use 31 for maritime queries.
41	Met Reports	Used for making reports of weather conditions to the met office.
42	Navigational Hazards	Used for issuing warnings of dangers to navigation. Equivalent to a *Securité* call.
43	Ship Position Reports	Used for **A**utomated **M**utual-assistance **V**essel **R**escue Service reports. AMVER is a world-wide tracking service operated by the US Coast Guard.

Telephone calls on Inmarsat A

Initiating a telephone call through a satellite is a two-stage process. When the mobile station first accesses the satellite with a request for a particular LES, the Network Co-ordinating Station allocates a free channel between the mobile station and the satellite and another free channel between the satellite and the LES. This takes only a few seconds and requires no intervention by the operator on board the vessel.

Once this link is established, the LES can complete the call and the link is made to the terrestrial telecommunication network or back up to the satellite if the call is to another mobile station.

The procedure for establishing a telephone link is:

1. Chose an appropriate LES and make sure that the antenna is locked on to a satellite that the chosen LES can use.
2. Select Routine Priority – Priority 0.
3. Lift telephone handset. When the dial tone heard enter the two-digit code for the chosen LES.
4. Select channel type – normally 'compander on' – code 1. Code 2 is used for sending data. Press 'return' or 'enter'.
5. The NCS will allocate the channels and as soon as it is satisfied with the links, another dial tone will be heard.
6. Enter service code – e.g. 00 for automatic dialling. At this point, the telephone number can be entered using the normal international dialling code for the country (44 for the UK, 1 for the USA etc.), followed by the area code (omitting any leading zeros) and the subscriber's number. When all the digits of the number have been entered, press # to indicate that the number is complete. Do not leave

any spaces if the number is entered using a keyboard. The subscriber's telephone should ring, and hopefully be answered!

Clearing the channel is simply a matter of 'hanging up'. The NCS will automatically release the channels for other stations to use.

Telex by Inmarsat A

The use of telex has some advantages over voice communications.

- Legally, a telex message can be regarded as a written document and there is a record of what has been sent.
- The message can be prepared ahead of transmission, so no important details are forgotten.
- Messages can be sent at any time – there need not be an operator present.
- Exchange of answerback codes at the beginning and end of the message effectively confirms receipt of the message.
- Messages can be sent by Store-and-Forward, where the message is stored on a computer at the LES, for later transmission to one or more addresses at a suitable time.

There are several telex services offered by most LESs and as with the telephone system there is a two-digit service code to select the required service. Where the same service is applicable to both telephone and telex the code is the same, for example code 38 will get you medical assistance by voice or by telex, depending on the mode in operation. There are some codes unique to telex:

15	Radio Telegram Service	Some LESs will accept a telex for onward transmission to non-satellite equipped ships as a radio telegram.
22	Store-and-Forward	This is usually a national service within the country where the LES is situated.
24	Telex Letter Service	Messages are sent from a vessel at sea by telex to be forwarded by the LES by mail.
91	Automatic Line Test	The LES will normally send the 'quick brown fox' message and the numbers 0–9.

Setting up a telex call is a two-stage process, very similar to initiating a telephone call.

1. Choose an appropriate LES and make sure that the antenna is locked on to a satellite that the chosen LES can use.
2. Select Routine Priority – Priority 0.
3. Select telex mode.
4. Enter the two-digit code for the chosen LES.
5. Enter channel code – compander on – code 1. Code 2 is for transmitting data.

87

6. Enter 1 to tell the NCS you are ready. The NCS will allocate suitable channels and when the link is established the LES will respond with a telex header – Date, Time, Identity, and GA+.
7. Enter service code – e.g. 00 for automatic dialling or 22 for Store-and-Forward, then the desired number, using the normal international *telex* dialling code for the country (remember these are different from the telephone codes, e.g. the UK is 51 for a telex call, not 44 as used for telephone calls) followed by the subscriber's number. If these numbers are entered from a keyboard, then do not put any spaces between the numbers.
8. Press+to indicate that the number is complete.
9. The call should be connected and if it is a direct telex, the subscriber's answerback will be received. (If you are sending a Store-and-Forward telex, you will get a GA+ from the LES.)
10. Press* to release your identity, and then send the text of your message.
11. Send WRU+ (**W**ho a**R**e yo**U**) to receive the subscriber's answerback code again. This effectively confirms receipt of the telex.
12. Terminate the connection by sending five stops ..... at the beginning of a line. This disconnects the link and advises you of the time of the transmission.

There are quite a lot of codes which are used in telex as a kind of shorthand. Most of the same codes are used in all forms of telex, whether it be by MF/HF or satellite. Some of the more common telex codes are included in Appendix V for reference.

Inmarsat C

Inmarsat C supports the transmission of data and data only. Voice transmission is not possible by Inmarsat C. It is a Store-and-Forward system. Two-way communications in 'real time' are not possible. The on-board terminal may be a stand-alone system or it may be interfaced to a **P**ersonal **C**omputer. In either case outgoing messages are normally entered through a keyboard and incoming ones displayed on a screen and/or printed on paper.

Inmarsat C supports **E**nhanced **G**roup **C**alling, which means that messages can be sent to selected groups of vessels or vessels in a particular area. This is a very important part of the safety aspect of GMDSS, for the dissemination of **M**aritime **S**afety **I**nformation.

Because the antenna for Inmarsat C is non-directional, at any given moment a shipboard terminal is able to communicate with any satellite which is more than 5 degrees above the horizon. The operator has to tell the on-board terminal with which satellite he wishes to communicate, and 'log on' to that satellite.

Technically, the transmission of messages between the vessel and the LES is much more complicated than with Inmarsat A or B. Fortunately, most of this is done without any action being taken by the on-board operator and in practice the system is extremely easy to use.

When a message has been prepared for transmission the on-board terminal requests a channel through the satellite. This is allocated by the **Network Co-ordination Station** by way of the requested LES, which remotely tunes the on-board terminal to the correct frequency. The on-board terminal then sends the message via the satellite to the LES in a series of data packets using a system called Time Division Multiplexing. Fortunately we do not need to understand how this works except that it enables up to 22 mobile stations to send or receive messages on the same frequency, via the same satellite, at the same time. Allowing several users to operate on each channel at the same time not only eases congestion problems but helps to keep the cost down.

Miraculously, the LES sorts out which packet of data is to go where and checks that all the packets have been correctly received. It asks for a repeat of any that are in doubt and re-assembles the message. The message can then be forwarded to a telex subscriber, an E-mail address, a shore-based fax machine, or to another vessel via any of the Inmarsat satellites.

Let's have a look how it all works in practice. The NCS for each satellite monitors one channel particular to that satellite. It is termed the Common Channel. For any mobile station to operate it must be synchronised with the Common Channel for that satellite and the terminal logged on to that particular Ocean Region.

The actual log-on procedure varies from terminal to terminal, and it will be detailed in the manual for the equipment. With most equipment it is just a matter of selecting the desired satellite from a menu, telling the set to initiate log on and waiting until it tells you that the log-on procedure is complete. Normally, once logged on the equipment is left to run, monitoring the Common Channel.

If the equipment is to be turned off for any reason, perhaps to conserve power on a small vessel, then the terminal must be logged off from the NCS otherwise an LES may waste a lot of time trying to get through to a set which is turned off. The LES could even assume that there is a problem with the vessel if it does not respond and possibly even initiate distress proceedings, so it is essential to log off before turning off. The same is true when changing Ocean Regions, or changing satellites to make use of a particular LES. You must log off from one NCS before trying to log on to another.

Distress calls on Inmarsat C

Most Inmarsat C terminals have a 'panic button'. Actually there are usually two buttons which require a simultaneous press to send a distress alert. Such a distress alert will take precedence over any other traffic and will automatically be routed to the Rescue Co-ordination Centre. Obviously, for the 'panic button' to work instantly the terminal must be logged on to the NCS for that Ocean Area – a good reason for always being logged on!

If the terminal is not logged on to an NCS and the 'panic button' is pressed, the equipment should automatically go through the log-on procedure and then send the distress alert. This presupposes that the vessel has not sunk in the interim!

As a minimum, the RCC will receive the vessel's identity and the fact that it is in distress. However most Inmarsat C terminals can, and should, be interfaced with a GPS navigation receiver, in which case the position will automatically be included.

This type of distress alert which gives no other information is called an 'undesignated distress alert' and should only be used if time is at an absolute premium. If there is just a little more time, more information can easily be included.

All terminals have the facility for sending a 'designated distress alert' and if time permits, this is preferable. With most terminals the process is just one of selecting options from the on-screen prompts.

1. Select Distress Alert.
2. Select nearest or most suitable LES.
3. Position – If not entered automatically by a GPS receiver, then enter it manually.
4. Date and time of position – May be entered automatically or manually.
5. Nature of distress. Options are:

Unspecified	Flooding	Grounding
Sinking	Abandoning Ship	Fire/explosion
Collision	Listing	Disabled and adrift

6. Course – Automatically or manually entered.
7. Speed – Automatically or manually entered.
8. Send the distress alert.
9. If no acknowledgement is received in 5 minutes, then transmit the alert again.

Once the distress alert has been acknowledged by the RCC, the distress message can be sent. Send the initial message in the MIPDANIO format, so all the essential information is sent. If time allows, this can be amplified in later messages, but get the essentials out first:

Mayday – Start the message with a Mayday or an SOS so the RCC is in no doubt that it is a distress situation.

Identity – Include name and call-sign of the vessel as well as the MMSI.

Position – If it was not included automatically, then give an updated position.

Distress – the nature of the distress may have been included if a 'designated alert' was sent. If an undesignated alert was sent, then the nature of the distress must be sent.

Assistance needed.

Number of persons on board.

Information – Any other information that might be of assistance to rescuers.

Over – The end of a message is usually indicated by an on screen prompt to send the message.

Urgency, Safety, and Routine calls on Inmarsat C

To send any type of message other than distress, it is usually a case of following the on-screen prompts and selecting the appropriate choice. On Inmarsat C there is a similar code to A for selecting the desired service. Since C cannot support voice communications, some of the services offered on A or B are not available on C. The principal codes for services available on C are:

15	Telegram	Sending a telegram to a shore address.
21	Telex Store-and-Forward	The message is forwarded to a shore telex number.
24	Radio Telex Letter	The message is forwarded by mail to a shore address.
31	Maritime Enquiries	Information regarding ship location or authorisation.
32	Medical Advice	The LES will connect you with a hospital or doctor, to get medical *advice*. (See 38 for assistance.)
33	Technical Assistance	Technical staff at the LES should normally be available to help with equipment problems.
38	Medical *Assistance*	For *urgent* medical assistance, such as medical evacuation or for a doctor to board the vessel. This is equivalent to a 'Pan Pan Medico' call. Use 32 for medical advice.
39	Maritime *Assistance*	For urgent assistance, such as needing a tow. Equivalent to a Pan Pan call.
41	Met Reports	Making reports of weather conditions to the met office.
42	Navigational Hazards	For issuing warnings of dangers to navigation. Equivalent to a *Securité* call.

| 43 | Ship Position Reports | Used for Automated Mutual-assistance Vessel Rescue Service reports. AMVER is a world-wide tracking service operated by the US Coast Guard. |
| 68 | Information Service | |

To place a call, make sure the terminal is logged on to the Ocean Region applicable to the LES which is best suited to handle your traffic. Prepare your message so that it is ready for sending, then initiate the call.

1. Select desired LES – This will either be a menu choice, or require the input of the appropriate code.
2. Select required service – Again, this will either be a menu choice or a code as above.
3. Send the message.
4. The LES will ask if there is further traffic and if not, the set will return to idle to monitor the common channel.

Do not forget to log off before turning off, or before changing to a different Ocean Region.

An Inmarsat B unit – voice only. It is not GMDSS approved (no EGC) but has a special distress function.

CHAPTER 10

Maritime Mobile Service Identity

The idea of the **M**aritime **M**obile **S**ervice **I**dentity is to give every vessel a unique number, which will be its identity not only for radio calls via DSC, but also to allow telephone or telex subscribers ashore to call the vessel automatically.

There are four kinds of MMSI:

1. Individual ship station identity – a number for calling a particular vessel.
2. Group ship identities – a number which allows a particular group of ships to be called at the same time, for example, all the yachts in a particular race or all the ships that belong to one company.
3. Individual Coast Station identity – a number for calling a particular Coast Station.
4. Group Coast Station identity – a number which allows all the Coast Stations of a particular group to be called at the same time.

As part of the nine-digit number which is assigned to each station, a three-digit code is included which indicates which country has issued that particular MMSI. The three-digit number indicating the country is called the Maritime Identification Digits.

The MID is allocated by the International Telecommunications Union and the current list of assigned MID numbers is maintained in Appendix 43 of the ITU Regulations. The United States' MID is 366, and for the UK it is 232 or 233.

Ship Station Identities
The MMSI for an individual vessel is made up of a nine-digit number in the format:

MIDXXXXXX

MID is the three-digit code which indicates the country that issued the MMSI and X is any figure from 0 to 9.

Group Ship Call Identities

The MMSI for a group of ships starts with a 0 before the MID. The MID only indicates the country which issued the MMSI, so not all the vessels in the group need necessarily be of the same nationality. The format for a group ship call MMSI is:

0MIDXXXXX

The first figure is always 0, MID is the three-digit code indicating the country issuing the MMSI and X is any number from 0 to 9.

Coast Station Identities

The MMSI number for any Coast Station starts with two zeros. So the format is:

00MIDXXXX

The first two numbers are zeros, MID indicates the country where the Coast Station is located and X is any number from 0 to 9. These last four numbers are the same as the Selcall number for the Coast Station.

Group Coast Station Identities

MMSIs for Coast Stations can be grouped together to allow simultaneous calling to several stations. For example, in the United States, all the Coast Guard Coast Stations have a group identity call of 003669999. So a DSC call using that MMSI will be received by any Coast Guard Station within radio range.

This system of allocation would work without problem if it were not for the shortcomings of many shore-based telephone and telex networks. In many cases the maximum number of digits that can be recognised or transmitted over the shore networks, for the purpose of determining the identity of a ship, is six. The number which the shore network uses to determine the ship's identity is called the Ship Station Number.

There are several methods which various countries use to modify the full nine-digit MMSI to make it into an acceptable Ship Station Number, which can be recognised by the shore-based network.

Vessels expecting to use automatic telephone facilities can be issued with a special MMSI, where the last three digits of the MMSI are three zeros. These three trailing zeros can be ignored by the shore telephone exchange, so that an MMSI of MIDXXX000 becomes a six-digit Ship Station Number of MIDXXX.

The drawback for this abbreviation is that each MID can only support 999 MMSIs so more MIDs would have to be issued as more vessels were allocated MMSIs.

If vessels are only going to operate in national waters and will not be making or receiving international calls, then the MID itself can be abbreviated to a 9. The MMSI issued has a single trailing zero which can be ignored by the telephone exchange. So a nine-digit MMSI number MIDXXXXX0 becomes a six-digit Ship Station Identity of 9XXXXX. With this format each MID can support 99,000 MMSIs on a national basis.

Ships using the Inmarsat satellite communication system also have to use identifying numbers. The original Inmarsat A system uses its own unique numbers to identify subscribers. These are nine-digit numbers but they bear no relationship to the MMSI numbers.

With the Inmarsat B,C and M systems the plan was for all users to be allocated MMSIs in the format MIDXXX000, but the problem is that with the increased popularity of satellite communications many countries are running out of MID numbers. The ITU Recommendations stipulate that ships using Inmarsat B,C and M be assigned a **M**aritime **E**arth **S**tation **I**dentity **N**umber in the format TMIDXXXYY.

T indicates the type of Inmarsat service: 0=Inmarsat A group call,
   3=Inmarsat B, 4=Inmarsat C, 6=Inmarsat M.
MIDXXX is the Ship Station number which relates to the allocated MMSI of
   MIDXXX000.
YY indicates an on-board extension. For example, 00 might ring on the bridge,
   01 could be in the Owner's accommodation and 02 might be a fax machine etc..

The MMSI was envisaged as a kind of universal phone number for each vessel. However, sheer weight of numbers threatens this concept and already there is talk of issuing Inmarsat identity numbers for all Inmarsat services, independent of the MMSIs.

To obtain an MMSI, application should be made to the national licensing authority and either a new licence will be issued or the old one endorsed. If you expect to receive automatic calls from ashore, then it is advisable to check that the issued number is of a format acceptable to the exchange which will be placing the calls.

The **I**nternational **T**elecommunications **U**nion, through their Maritime Mobile Access Retrieval System, maintains a database which gives a list of all the MID numbers allocated to a country and contains information regarding each vessels' MMSI and call-sign.

CHAPTER 11

Enhanced Group
Calling and the
SafetyNET

afetyNET is a world-wide system for the broadcast of **Maritime Safety**
Information, administered by the International Maritime **Organisation**.
Enhanced Group Calling allows the MSI to be sent only to concerned
vessels without every vessel in the world having to sift through every piece of
information. The system can select a specific group of vessels, or more often
in the case of safety information, vessels in a particular area. Such an area can
be:

- a particular 'Navarea' or 'Metarea', of which there are 16 in the world
- for all vessels within a circular area – a stipulated number of miles from a given
  position
- a rectangular area – within a given distance north and east from a particular position.

When the message is transmitted, a code indicating who should receive it
is incorporated into the beginning of the message. The EGC receiver exam-
ines the code and automatically recognises if it is supposed to receive the
message. Any messages not meant for that receiver are ignored.

Additionally, each message incorporates a serial number so that the
receiver knows whether or not it has already received that message, in which
case it does not print the duplicate. For this reason, if for no other, it is advisable to leave the equipment running.

SafetyNET messages include:

1. Shore-to-ship distress alert relays. These are normally sent to circular areas,
   centred on the position of the distressed vessel.

2. Search-and-rescue co-ordination messages. These are normally sent to vessels in a specified area.
3. Urgency messages and navigational warnings.
4. Meteorological and navigational warnings. Normally sent to vessels in a particular NAVAREA.
5. Coastal warnings. Issued to vessels in coastal areas not covered by Navtex, notably much of the Australian coast.

Additionally, national administrations may send messages to areas adjoining their shores, covering the same categories as above.

Very few Inmarsat terminals can receive a SafetyNET message if they are transmitting when the message is being broadcast, so each message is normally repeated after a six-minute delay to allow a second chance at receiving it. Although reception of the messages is usually automatic, lists and schedules of SafetyNET broadcasts are published so the operator can ensure that the terminal is logged on to the appropriate satellite at the time when the messages are being broadcast.

To receive the applicable SafetyNET messages:

1. For Inmarsat C, log on to the Ocean Area for which the desired information will be broadcast. For Inmarsat A, ensure that the antenna is locked on to the applicable satellite. In some areas, notably much of Europe, it is possible to access the AOR-W, AOR-E, and IOR satellites, all from the same location. However, forecasts and warnings for the particular area of interest might only be broadcast from one satellite and you have to be logged on to, or have the antenna pointed at, that satellite to receive the broadcast.
2. Select the appropriate Navarea identification code for the area of interest, or, when off the Australian coast, the particular coastal area code.
3. Enter the vessel's position. If this is not done automatically, through an interface to a GPS, then the position must be entered manually every four hours. If the position is not updated within 12 hours, then the terminal will stop being selective for messages as to area, and it will print out all messages received, which can be overwhelming!

FleetNET is the commercial equivalent of SafetyNET. Once again, messages can be addressed to vessels by group such as the participants in a race or vessels belonging to one company, or less commonly, vessels in a particular region. Most of the services offered are for subscribers only and can include information such as news services or financial information.

CHAPTER 12

Navtex

Navtex is an international system for the standardised broadcast and reception of **M**arine **S**afety **I**nformation, adopted by the **I**nternational **M**aritime **O**rganisation. Around the world, the Navtex broadcasts are transmitted in English on a frequency of 518 kHz in the MF band. This gives a useful range of up to about 400 miles. Broadcasts are arranged in such a way that adjacent stations transmit their information at different times, to reduce the chance of them interfering with each other. The power of each station is set with reference to the distance between the various stations, to ensure continuous coverage, but minimal interference.

Some countries transmit the MSIs in their own language and this is done on a frequency of 490 kHz, or sometimes on 578 kHz. Additionally, there is a limited service on HF for those vessels in GMDSS areas A 3 and A 4 which are not equipped with satellite communication, but which can receive telex messages. The principal frequency used is 4209.5 kHz.

Regardless of the frequency, the messages are transmitted by **SI**mplex **T**elex **O**ver **R**adio, or Narrow Band Direct Printing as it is sometimes called. Since the messages are being sent to a large number of stations at the same time, they are transmitted in the **F**orward **E**rror **C**orrection mode (see the section on telex for an explanation of how FEC works).

For the MF broadcasts, a dedicated Navtex receiver is normally used. Such a receiver usually incorporates its own printer or sometimes a screen to display the received messages. These sets are small, self-contained, and draw very little power and so are suitable for use on virtually any size of vessel. HF broadcasts are usually received on the ship's HF set and displayed by means of a telex terminal, or through a computer.

All the Navtex broadcasts are formatted in the same way. Each message is preceded with ZCZC, which is the phasing signal that enables the receiver to decode the message correctly. This signal is followed by a header consisting of two letters and two numbers.

The first letter after the phasing signal indicates the identity of the transmitter that is sending the message. All dedicated Navtex receivers can be programmed to receive messages only from selected stations. This is done by indicating the letter of the station or stations of interest. Transmissions from all other stations are ignored. Stations identified by the same letter are normally sited far enough apart to prevent reception of messages from the wrong one, or interference between the two. As far as possible, stations are numbered A to Z going in an anti-clockwise direction around each continent. The exception is Australia, where they are labelled in a clockwise direction – it must be something to do with the way the water goes down the plug-hole in the southern hemisphere!

The second letter of the header indicates the category of the message. There are seventeen of these:

A   Navigational warnings
B   Meteorological warnings
C   Ice reports
D   Search and rescue information
E   Meteorological forecasts
F   Pilot service messages
G   Decca messages
H   Loran messages
I   Omega messages
J   Satellite navigation messages
K   Other electronic nav-aid messages
L   Navigation warnings additional to A
V   Special services, such as notices to fishermen
W   National messages, such as environmental reports
X   Special services allocated by IMO Navtex panel
Y   Special services allocated by IMO Navtex panel
Z   No messages on hand.

The receiver can be programmed to receive only those categories of message which are of concern to the operator. For example, if the vessel does not have Decca fitted, messages concerning the Decca system are of little interest. Desired message categories are selected by keying in the appropriate letters. Messages of all other categories are ignored, except that messages in categories A,B, D and L cannot be rejected and will always be received. This is to ensure that no important safety, weather, or distress alerts are missed.

The two numbers in the message header are the serial number of each individual message. If the receiver is left turned on, it remembers which messages have already been received. Duplicate messages are not printed.

Each station normally transmits the current MSIs three times a day, that is every eight hours. The actual time of transmission is indicated in the appropriate list of radio signals, and the times are arranged to avoid interference between stations that could simultaneously be in range of a vessel.

Messages which are classed as 'vital' will be broadcast immediately, ahead of schedule, subject only to avoiding interference. Messages classed as 'important' will be broadcast at the next period when the frequency is unused. Both types of messages will be repeated at the next scheduled broadcast with the 'routine' messages. If the times of transmission are not known, as long as the set is turned on at least eight hours before a voyage commences the operator should be in possession of all the current MSIs.

When a set is first installed, or when changing from one area to another, it is important to select the identities of the station or stations from which you want to receive MSIs. If, for some reason, the identities of the stations are not known, then select all stations and leave the set turned on for eight hours. It will then receive all the stations within range. Do this by day, otherwise the increased range by night will bring messages from what seems like half the world. To reduce the number of incoming messages, select only A, B, D and L messages. After eight hours, it will be possible to see which stations are in range and then to select which one or ones that you want to monitor. Then you can choose the message categories that you want, and after that the chosen messages should be received automatically. All you have to do then is to read the messages!

The Navtex receiver usually has a self-test facility. The operator's handbook should explain how to perform any available tests. These should be done on a weekly basis and the results logged.

CHAPTER 13

EPIRBS

E mergency Position Indicating Radio Beacons have been with us for a
number of years. Their name explains their function. EPIRBs are used
for transmitting a distress alert and then for guiding the rescuers to
the site. An operating EPIRB indicates that one or more persons are in distress and that they may or may not have the ability to receive radio transmissions.

Types of EPIRBs

The earliest EPIRBs transmitted on the aircraft emergency frequencies of
121.5 MHz and/or 243 MHz. They simply transmitted a signal, usually an
alternating tone, to be received on the emergency frequency on a normal aircraft radio – 121.5 MHz being the civil emergency frequency, and 243 MHz
the military equivalent. Indeed, their early development was more for aircraft than for ships. For some reason, if they are fitted to aircraft, they are
know as **Emergency Location Transponders**. As this name suggests, they
were not thought of as a way to raise the alarm but more as a way to find the
distressed aircraft or ship. Such a beacon could only be used to raise the
alarm if an aircraft happened to pass within range and had its radio tuned to
the right frequency.

With the dawning of the space age this concept changed. It was realised
that if there was a satellite, or better still several satellites listening on these
frequencies, then an EPIRB could be used to raise the alarm in a distress situation and it soon became apparent that the position of the transmitting
beacon could be fixed from the satellite with a fair degree of accuracy.

In 1979, the then-USSR signed a treaty of co-operation with the USA,
Canada and France, to establish a satellite system to aid in search and
rescue. Cospas-Sarsat was born. Cospas is an acronym for the Russian words
meaning Space System for the Search of Vessels in Distress, and Sarsat is the
acronym for **S**earch **A**nd **R**escue **SAT**ellite. Trials began in 1982 and the

system was declared operational in 1985. In 1990, Russia assumed responsibility for the former Soviet segment.

There is always a minimum of four satellites in the system. The Russians keep at least two operational satellites in near polar orbits, at an altitude of about 1,000 kilometres. Each carries equipment for detecting and analysing EPIRB transmissions on 121.5 and 406 MHz. Additionally, there are always at least two US NOAA weather satellites which are in sun-synchronous near-polar orbits at an altitude of about 850 kilometres, each carrying a set of Search And Rescue instruments provided by Canada and France, also monitoring both frequencies.

From its inception, the Cospas-Sarsat system was designed to monitor two frequencies. The frequency of 121.5 MHz was retained for two reasons. Existing EPIRBs could use the system, and search aircraft would still be able to use their VHF radio equipment to home in on the victim's signal from a 121.5 MHz EPIRB. An additional higher frequency of 406 MHz was assigned for specialised satellite EPIRBs. This higher frequency could be made more stable, which makes fixing the position from the satellite much easier. The signal on this frequency incorporates a coded message to provide identification of the vessel to whom the EPIRB is licensed. The best EPIRB would be one that can transmit on both frequencies – 406 MHz to give the satellite the best chance of getting a good fix on the EPIRB's position and 121.5 MHz for any searching aircraft to home on.

On the ground there are some 22 Local User Terminals located in various countries. Each of these monitors each satellite as it passes. If a satellite detects an EPIRB signal and it is within 'sight' of an LUT, it will immediately relay the information to that ground station. If there is no LUT within range and the satellite receives a 406 MHz signal, then the satellite can store the information and transmit it to the first LUT that comes into range. It is not able to do this for signals received on 121.5 MHz. If the satellite is not in range of a LUT when it receives a 121.5 MHz signal it will not be relayed. This effectively limits the use of 121.5 MHz EPIRBs via the satellites to a range of about 1,600 miles from any LUT. With the 22 available LUTs much of the world is covered, but there are some gaps, particularly in the Southern Ocean from where the signal will not be relayed.

Because these satellites are in a comparatively low orbit – compare these altitudes with those of the Inmarsats at 36,000 kilometres – they can receive relatively low powered transmissions. An average 406 MHz EPIRB transmits with a power of about five watts and a 121.5 MHz EPIRB is usually under one watt. This means that the EPIRBs can be small because they do not require great big batteries to power them.

Each satellite completes an orbit about every 100 minutes. The satellite will pass from horizon to horizon in about 15 minutes. During its orbit each satellite can receive signals from a swathe some 400 kilometres wide. As the earth turns beneath the satellites they each pass over a new strip every orbit. The maximum delay that a distressed vessel should experience in waiting for a satellite to pass within range is about 90 minutes.

When it is activated, a 406 MHz EPIRB transmits a short coded message every 50 seconds. Each half-second burst indicates the identity of the vessel to whom the EPIRB is registered, but like the transmissions on 121.5 MHz it is still a very simple signal from a relatively unsophisticated transmitter. It is the satellite that does all the clever stuff.

When the satellite detects a signal on either frequency it monitors the signal, measuring its frequency very accurately. Because of the speed of the satellite, and the low orbit enhances this effect, the frequency appears to change due to the Doppler Effect. This is the same effect that makes a train whistle sound as if it is changing pitch as the train comes towards us and then passes.

The satellite is able to calculate the position of the EPIRB by measuring the Doppler shift. There is one slight problem. The calculation will produce two positions – one the mirror of the other, either side of the satellite's track. For a transmission on 121.5 MHz, the satellite will probably have to wait until the next pass to solve the ambiguity. Trouble starts if the next orbit does not pass close enough to the EPIRB to receive the signal. If this happens, the whole process has to start again with the next satellite.

The signal from a 406 MHz EPIRB is much more stable, allowing more accurate measurements to be taken. The satellite resolves the ambiguity by doing an extra calculation taking the rotation of the earth into consideration. For 90% of the 406 MHz signals it receives, the satellite can fix the position of the EPIRB to within about five kilometres (a little over 2.5 miles) with only one pass. By comparison, the probable error in the position fix for a 121.5 MHz EPIRB is about seventeen kilometres (about 9 miles) and even at that it is likely to take two passes of the satellite to achieve the fix.

The Cospas-Sarsat system can process up to ninety 406 MHz beacons which are activated at the same time – the mind boggles at what could cause such an occurrence! They are limited to handling a maximum of ten 121.5 MHz beacons simultaneously, but this limitation is unlikely to be a problem too often.

The Cospas-Sarsat organisation is currently experimenting with a 406 MHz payload on a geostationary satellite. This would have the advantage of instant alerting – no waiting for a satellite to come over the horizon. But a geostationary satellite cannot, with present technology, fix the position of an

EPIRB by examining the signal. The EPIRB would have to broadcast its position to the satellite, perhaps using a built-in GPS receiver.

This is exactly the technique adopted by the Inmarsat E EPIRBs. They operate on one of the normal Inmarsat frequencies of 1.6 GHz. The EPIRB must either be programmed with its position, or more normally, they contain an integrated GPS receiver. This makes the unit more expensive and bigger than a 406 MHz unit. Because they are transmitting a much more complicated message, and it has to travel 36,000 kilometres instead of a mere 850–1,000 kilometres, they must be much more powerful. This also makes them bigger and more expensive. The benefit is that the alert is near enough instantaneous and, as well as an accurate position, other information can be included in the message to assist any rescuers.

Compulsory GMDSS vessels must carry an EPIRB as part of the equipment list. For vessels limited to Area A1, this can be a VHF EPIRB. For vessels in any of the other areas A2, 3, and 4, it must be an EPIRB which can work through one of the satellite systems. Both the Cospas-Sarsat 406 MHz and the Inmarsat E EPIRBs are approved by the GMDSS.

Operation of EPIRBs and Test Procedures

For compulsory vessels, the EPIRB must be fitted in a 'float free' mounting. In such a mounting the EPIRB is held in place by a **Hydrostatic Release Unit**. This senses the increasing water pressure if a vessel sinks and at a predetermined depth the HRU releases the mount, allowing the EPIRB to float to the surface. A well designed mount will also cause the EPIRB to switch itself on as it is released, so it will start to operate automatically if the vessel sinks. For non-compulsory vessels such a mount is good to have, in case the vessel sinks very quickly before anybody has time to get the EPIRB from its stowage.

EPIRBs should be examined for physical damage on a weekly basis. If the EPIRB is retained in its mount by an HRU, then the expiration date or service date on the HRU should be noted. The expiration date of the EPIRB's battery should also be noted. This is usually given on the maker's label or another plate affixed to the EPIRB. Most EPIRBs have a test switch. This should be operated on a weekly basis or in accordance with the manufacturer's recommendations. The test switch is usually spring loaded so it cannot be left on inadvertently and thus flatten the battery. A light will indicate that the test circuits are operating correctly. For compulsory vessels these tests must be logged each week.

When operating a self-test, no signals are radiated and the EPIRB must not be tested by actual operation. If it is accidentally activated in the transmit mode, then it should be turned off at once and the false alarm cancelled by calling the nearest Coast Station and by making a safety call on the VHF radio for the benefit of any vessels in the vicinity.

When used in an emergency, some EPIRBs must be floating in the water for their antenna to operate at peak efficiency. The maker's instructions will say if their EPIRB should be operating afloat or if it can be kept inside the liferaft.

In either event, once the EPIRB is activated in a distress situation leave it switched on until the batteries are exhausted or until you have been rescued. There have been many cases reported where people kept turning the EPIRB on and off in an attempt to prolong the life of the battery. As we have already seen, except for an Inmarsat E EPIRB there can be a considerable delay before a satellite passes close enough to receive the signal from an EPIRB. If the satellite needs two passes to fix the position and the operator has turned the EPIRB off before the second pass, at best it will delay the satellite from fixing the position. It could also cause an unnecessary inaccuracy in the calculated position or even cause the satellite to dismiss the signal as erroneous. Once you have turned it on, leave it on.

A new development, which as yet is not part of the GMDSS, is the **STA**tus **REC**ording System. STAREC is somewhat akin to the 'Black Box' system of aircraft. It is being developed to explain the mysteries of vessels which vanish without trace.

The STAREC unit is interfaced with various sensors mounted in the vessel and it records their readings at regular intervals. It retains the last several hours of readings, replacing the earliest recordings with the latest. The unit is self-contained with its own position fixing system and its own Inmarsat C terminal.

In a distress situation the unit can either be jettisoned or it can float free, and on activation it will automatically contact a pre-programmed station. This could be a **R**escue **C**o-ordination **C**entre or the perhaps the Owner's office. The unit will transmit a brief message, basically saying that it has been activated. It can then be interrogated and all the recorded data down-loaded without the unit itself having to be located or retrieved. All relative systems on board the ship can be monitored and the recorded data should explain what went wrong when the distress situation arose. In the future, these units may well become GMDSS compulsory for some vessels.

CHAPTER 14

Search And Rescue Transponders

S earch And Rescue Transponders are electronic units which react to the emissions of X-band radars. Each time a SART detects a pulse from an X-band radar it transmits a signal which is displayed on the screen of the radar which activated it. This can greatly help a would-be rescuer to locate a liferaft. They can be thought of as 'active' radar reflectors as they electronically enhance the echo received by a radar.

All compulsory GMDSS vessels up to 500 tons must carry at least one SART. Above 500 tons, they must carry two. Non-compulsory vessels are strongly advised to carry at least one to aid in any possible rescue.

Operation of SARTs and Test Procedures

How do they work? A SART has a receiver which scans for UHF signals between 9.2 and 9.5 GHz – the frequencies on which an X-band radar transmits its signal. As soon as the SART detects a signal it immediately transmits its own signal on the same frequency. This signal consists of a series of twelve pulses, and these are displayed on the screen of the radar as a series of twelve echoes with a gap of 0.6 miles between each of them. The first dot is at the position of the SART, with the remainder radiating in a straight line towards the edge of the screen.

As the rescue vessel approaches the SART, the twelve dots each become short arcs. These arcs increase in size as the vessel gets closer, until the signal from the SART is permanently activated by the weakest side-lobes from the radar transmission. The signal from the SART becomes twelve concentric circles on the radar screen and this tells the would-be rescuers that they have more or less arrived.

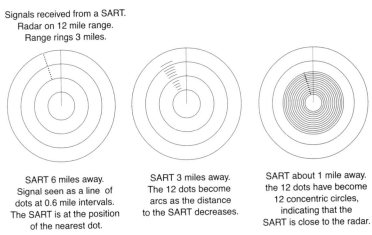

Signals received from a SART.
Radar on 12 mile range.
Range rings 3 miles.

SART 6 miles away.
Signal seen as a line of
dots at 0.6 mile intervals.
The SART is at the position
of the nearest dot.

SART 3 miles away.
The 12 dots become
arcs as the distance
to the SART decreases.

SART about 1 mile away.
the 12 dots have become
12 concentric circles,
indicating that the
SART is close to the radar.

Fig 14.1 SART signals received at long, medium and short ranges

When a SART is switched on it will show a light to indicate that it is working. An approved SART should have sufficient power to operate in this stand-by mode for at least 96 hours. When it receives a signal from an X-band radar, and transmits its own signal, it will either flash this indicating light or in some cases a second light or even a buzzer. This will serve to let the distressed persons know that an approaching radar is activating the SART. If the survivors have a handheld VHF with them then this would be a good time to use it to try calling the approaching ship.

Since the radar UHF signals can only effectively travel in a straight line, the distance from which a SART can be activated by a radar is dependent on its own height and the height of the interrogating radar scanner. Most SARTs have an extendible handle to help in positioning it as high as possible in the liferaft or lifeboat. The SART must be secured outside the canopy of the liferaft. Operating it from inside the liferaft will greatly reduce its effectiveness. The International Maritime Organisation stipulates that a SART mounted at a height of one metre must be detectable by a ship's radar with a scanner height of 15 metres at a distance of at least 5 miles.

It has been found from tests that a ship's radar will usually detect a SART laying flat on the floor of a liferaft at around 1.8 miles. If the SART is upright on the floor the detection range increases to about 2.5 miles. It should be possible, under most conditions, to mount the SART at least two metres high. A normal detection range for a SART mounted two metres above sea level by an average ship's radar is about seven to ten miles. However, a search aircraft equipped with an X-band radar should be able to detect it from at least 30 miles when flying at an altitude of around 3,000 feet.

All SARTs should be checked on a weekly basis for any physical damage and for the expiration date of the battery. This is normally indicated on the manufacturer's plate affixed to the SART. It is permitted to check the operation of a SART by briefly turning it on and exposing it to the transmissions of the ship's radar. If this is done on board, then the radar screen will be flooded with the concentric circles, showing the proximity of the SART. Such tests should be conducted on a monthly basis and should be kept short so as not to shorten the life of the battery too much and to reduce the risk of other vessels seeing it, resulting in a false distress alert. Ideally, such tests should be conducted when there are no other vessels within radar range so as not to cause interference or false alarms.

Vessels which are using their radar to look for a SART should use a range of 6 or 12 miles on the radar for optimum results. If a shorter range is selected, the narrower bandwidth used in the receiver will reduce the brightness of the dots making them harder to see. There is no point in using a longer range, since the maximum distance a SART will be detectable from another vessel is 7 to 10 miles.

There are some SARTs which have a so-called anti-collision mode. When operated in this mode they transmit five pulses instead of the normal twelve. Such a unit may well help the radar operator on an approaching ship to see you, but there is a danger that it might be mistaken for the distress signal and the ship may possibly try to rescue you, even if you were not in distress. Such use of a SART is not encouraged.

Under distress conditions though, there is no doubt that a SART is a valuable aid for any vessel to carry. It will greatly facilitate any search and rescue operation.

SART with handle for mounting on a liferaft. A flashing light and buzzer indicate when it is sending a signal to a radar.

CHAPTER 15

Telegrams by Radio

Ashore, telegrams have almost died a death. Faxes and E-mail have all but driven them into extinction. However, telegrams can be sent over the radio and it is not necessary to have a telex machine on board – telegrams can be dictated to a Coast Station over a normal voice link. A GMDSS operator has to know the basics for sending a telegram via a Coast Station. This could be done by VHF, MF, HF or even satellite.

Procedures for sending Telegrams by Radio

A radio telegram is made up of four parts: Preamble, Address, Text of the message and the Signature – if any.

The Preamble

The preamble must contain:

* The name of the vessel sending the telegram.
* The serial number of the telegram. Telegrams are numbered sequentially for each Coast Station worked, starting with number 1 at midnight.
* The number of words – chargeable and actual. Words, or groups of characters or numbers, not exceeding 10 characters are charged as one word. Any words or groups of characters or numbers, in excess of 10 characters are charged as one word for each 10 characters or part thereof. So 'telephone' would be charged as one word, but 'telephoning' would be charged as two. The number of chargeable words is written first, followed by the actual number of words, e.g. 17/14.
* The date and time that the telegram was presented for transmission.
* Service instructions – if any. This could include 'urgent', or some stations may offer a 'greetings telegram' service.

The Address

The address must contain everything that is needed to effect delivery. This could be a postal address, in which the name and full street and town address must be included. If the telegram is to go via a telegraphic office, then the address of that office should be written as it appears in the list of Telegraphic Offices. If it is to be delivered by telephone, then the address should be preceded with the letters TF followed by the full telephone number, the name of the recipient, and the town. For delivery by telex, the address should begin with TLX, followed immediately by the telex number and the name of the recipient.

The Text

Each telegram must contain at least one character of text. It is possible to send a telegram with a text of just one letter, which could convey a special meaning to the recipient. The text must consist of normal Latin characters, the numbers 1 to 0, and the usual punctuation marks.

The Signature

A signature is not compulsory, but may be written in any form.

A radio telegram should, whenever possible, be sent by telex. There is less likelihood of errors if the message is written. However, a telegram can be sent by telephony but care should be taken to repeat, or phonetically spell, any difficult words. Any complex numbers should be repeated and the standard phonetic alphabet and numerals should be used.

The radio operator should not consider the radio telegram 'cleared' until an acknowledgement of receipt has been obtained from the Coast Station.

CHAPTER 16

Basic Electrical Theory

A ny source of electricity has a certain voltage. In a house it is 240 volts or 110 volts depending on the national supplier of the country concerned. Such a supply will be Alternating Current, where there is no constant positive and negative voltage, but rather a 'live' terminal and a neutral. The live terminal will be constantly alternating between being positive to the neutral terminal and negative to it.

Although most vessels will use alternating current on board for domestic services, as far as our GMDSS equipment is concerned all or most of it will be powered by Direct Current. With any direct current, one terminal is always positive (+) and the other is always negative (−). The DC supply will be at a particular voltage, in our case normally 12 or 24 volts. The voltage indicates the potential the supply has for delivering power.

Introduction to Voltage, Current and Resistance in electrical circuits

Let's stop for a moment to imagine a waterwheel, which is going to be used to turn some piece of machinery. The wheel is turned by water coming out of the end of a pipe, and hitting the paddles on the wheel. Two factors control how much power the wheel can generate – the force of the water and the volume of water reaching the wheel. Obviously water dropping a hundred feet onto the wheel will generate more power than water dropping just a few inches. Likewise, 500 gallons per minute rushing over the wheel will generate more power than 3 or 4 gallons trickling over it.

In electrical terms, the height that the water has to drop is equivalent to the voltage of the supply and how much water flows over the wheel is equivalent

111

to the current. (Electrical current is measured in amperes.) Just as the power generated by the waterwheel is the product of the height of the supply multiplied by the volume of water, so too in electrical terms power is measured by multiplying the voltage by the current. Voltage is usually indicated by V and current, in amperes, by I. So we can say that power=V×I.

We would expect the units of power to be volt amps, and indeed one often sees a generator rated as so many kva (kilovolt amps), but the normal unit of power is watts. One watt=1 volt amp. One kilowatt=1,000 watts.

The symbol for power is W, so now we can write:

$$W=V×I$$

If we know any two of the three terms we can calculate the third. For example if we know the voltage and can measure the current, we can calculate the power. Similarly, if we know the rated power of a piece of equipment and know the voltage, we can calculate the current that the equipment will draw:

$$I=W÷V$$

This is important, because we can see that for a given power output, if the voltage supply drops the current increases. If for example we have a radio transmitting at 100 watts using a 24-volt battery:

$$I=100÷24=4.17 \text{ amps.}$$

If the batteries are getting low, and their voltage has dropped to say 15 volts, for the radio to use the same 100 watts of power the current must increase:

$$I=100÷15=6.66 \text{ amps.}$$

The current has risen by over 50%, which not only means that the battery will be flattened even quicker but the increased current may be sufficient to damage some components inside the radio or to perhaps blow the fuse which is installed to protect the radio. It is important for the operator to continually monitor the supply voltage for any equipment, as it is very easy to damage the equipment or to blow fuses by operation at substantially lower voltages than specified.

Ohm's Law

There is one last little formula we should look at and this is Ohm's Law. Any piece of equipment, or indeed any electrical conductor, resists the flow of an electrical current. The resistance of a conductor restricts how much current can flow – the greater the resistance, the less current will flow.

Resistance is measured in Ohms. The electrical symbol is Ω, but in formulae, resistance is usually written as R. Ohm's law is usually written as:

$$V = I \times R.$$

Once again, if any two terms are known, the third can be calculated. For our use, the formula is more useful if we rearrange it as:

$$I = V \div R.$$

If we have a piece of equipment with a resistance of say 10Ω, with a 24 volt supply, then:

$$I = 24 \div 10 = 2.4 \text{ amps.}$$

If there is a short circuit inside that equipment and the resistance drops to perhaps 2Ω, then:

$$I = 24 \div 2 = 12 \text{ amps.}$$

Hopefully, this five-fold increase in current will blow the fuse and protect the equipment from further damage.

Fuses on board will usually be of the type enclosed in a small glass tube with metal end caps. Between the two caps, inside the tube, there is a thin strand of wire. This wire is able to carry a particular current without melting. The number of amps that it can withstand is usually indicated on the glass tube or on the end caps. If that specified current is exceeded, the wire melts and so isolates the equipment from the supply.

Fuses which are designed to carry large currents are usually encased in a ceramic material rather than glass. However, they too contain a wire which melts if it is overloaded and they work in exactly the same way as the small glass fuses.

An alternative to the fuse is a circuit breaker which can be re-set. The circuit breaker measures the current flowing through it, usually by measuring the heat that the current generates. If the set limit is exceeded, then the breaker opens so isolating the equipment. The breaker can be re-set when the problem has been solved, but it may need to cool before it can be re-set.

CHAPTER 17

Batteries

Much of the GMDSS equipment on board is powered by batteries. It is not only in the operator's own interest to make sure that they are maintained in good condition but it is his duty to look after them. For a compulsory GMDSS vessel the operator must make regular tests of the various batteries and must log the results of the tests.

Batteries store electrical energy in the form of chemical energy. When electricity is drawn from a battery, a chemical reaction occurs inside the battery. The battery will continue to produce electricity until all the chemicals have been used. On any vessel there will be two types of batteries, primary and secondary.

Primary batteries are non-rechargeable, such as are found in a SART or EPIRB. They will have an expiration date and at that date, or if used, they must be replaced with new batteries. Secondary batteries are rechargeable. After use, or after prolonged storage, these batteries can be recharged to restore their capacity. Charging reverses the chemical process inside the battery so the battery can once again supply electricity. Secondary batteries are found in handheld VHFs, stand-by emergency batteries and, particularly on smaller vessels or yachts, secondary batteries will power the main radio systems.

Most batteries are made from a series of individual cells. Every battery, and indeed every cell making up a battery, has a positive (marked +) and a negative (marked −) terminal and each cell has a nominal voltage. The nominal voltage of a cell or battery is its average operating voltage. The voltage can be much higher when the battery is being charged and considerably lower than the nominal voltage when the battery is almost discharged. How many volts the nominal voltage is depends on the chemical composition of the cell. For example, a normal car battery is made using lead/acid cells. A lead/acid cell will always have a nominal voltage of 2 volts. When it is fully charged, the voltage could be as much as 2.4 volts and when it is almost discharged it could drop to 1.8 volts, or even less.

In a car battery, to reduce the current drawn by the starter-motor to reasonable levels we need a higher voltage than 2 volts. Six of these cells are connected in series. That is, they are joined together in a string, the positive of one cell connected to the negative of the next and so on. This results in the battery as a whole having a nominal voltage of 12 volts. We could just as easily join two 12-volt batteries in series to give us, in effect, one 24-volt battery if that is the voltage that is required.

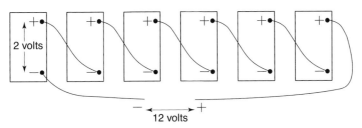

Fig 17.1 12-volt battery consisting of six 2-volt cells in series

How much power a battery can store is called the capacity of the battery. The capacity of a battery is measured by how much current, measured in amperes, it can supply for how many hours. The units are Ampere hours (Ah). By joining cells or batteries together in parallel, joining positive to positive and negative to negative, the capacity of the battery as a whole is the sum of the capacity of the individual batteries.

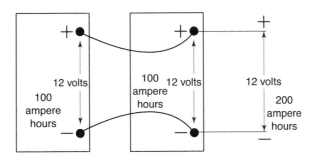

Fig 17.2 Two batteries connected in parallel

Primary (non-rechargeable) batteries can be used in series to achieve a particular voltage. For example, two or more batteries are often used in series, i.e. positive to negative in a flashlight to allow a bulb of higher voltage to be used. This will give a brighter light without having to draw a heavier

115

current. However, primary batteries should never be used in parallel because there is a possibility of one battery trying to recharge another.

Secondary cells can be used in series, in parallel, or in a combination of both to achieve the voltage and capacity that is required. The only limitation being that each cell is of a similar voltage, capacity and chemical composition.

All batteries will lose part of their capacity to produce electricity while they are waiting to be used. They suffer a chemical process other than the main electricity-producing reaction. This is a self-destructive reaction which slowly uses the chemicals which are needed for the electricity-producing reaction. This results in a steady loss of capacity or loss of charge. How much energy is lost per year varies with the type of cell that is used in the battery.

Primary, Non-rechargeable Batteries

There are five common types of primary, non-rechargeable batteries that we may find on board.

Carbon/zinc batteries

Carbon/zinc are the basic type of flashlight batteries. They have a nominal voltage of 1.5 volts per cell. Their advantage is that they are cheap but they tend to lose about 15% of their power per year just by sitting there. They must never be left inside equipment when they are exhausted, as they are liable to leak very corrosive chemicals which can cause expensive damage to the equipment. On board, they are only likely to be found in flashlights.

Alkaline manganese batteries

These are the premium 'longer life' batteries such as 'Duracell'. They too have a nominal voltage of 1.5 volts per cell. They are considerably more expensive than carbon/zinc batteries, but they have about 3 times the capacity and normally lose only about 7% of their capacity per year in storage. Both carbon/zinc and alkaline batteries can recover a little after a rest. If the battery is getting low, then by turning the equipment off for a while and letting the battery rest the useful life can be prolonged. Continuous discharge reduces the capacity of the battery. These batteries might also be found in flashlights and may form the basis of battery packs for EPIRBs or SARTS.

Mercury batteries

Mercury cells have a nominal voltage of about 1.4 volts per cell. Once again they are more expensive, but they have as much as 6 to 8 times the capacity of carbon/zinc batteries and they lose only some 6% of their capacity per year in storage. Because of the environmental problems associated with the disposal of mercury batteries, they are used less frequently now.

Silver oxide batteries

These are familiar as the little round silver coloured batteries found in watches and calculators. The nominal voltage is around 1.5 volts per cell. They have a capacity similar to the alkaline manganese batteries, at considerably greater cost, but their big advantage is that they only lose about 4% of their capacity per year in storage. Apart from calculators and watches they can be found as back-up batteries for memory circuits in some equipment.

Lithium batteries

These are the most modern, high power batteries. Their voltage can vary from 1.5 to over 3 volts, depending on the construction. Their capacity is approaching that of the mercury batteries, but best of all, they generally lose less than 2% of their capacity per year. They are ideally suited as back-up batteries inside equipment because of their long service life. They may also be found in some of the more expensive EPIRBs and SARTs.

The operator should be aware of which equipment contains primary batteries and they should be checked regularly for leakage and must be replaced in accordance with the expiration dates given by the manufacturers.

Secondary, Rechargeable Batteries

Rechargeable cells also come in a variety of types. In all of them, electrical energy is stored by a reversible chemical reaction. There are four kinds that we might encounter.

Lead/acid batteries

This is the most common type of large rechargeable battery. This is the same as the ubiquitous car battery. Each battery is made from a number of individual cells, each having a nominal voltage of 2 volts.

117

Most batteries are made with 3 or 6 cells giving a battery voltage of 6 or 12 volts. These batteries are then grouped together to make a bank of the required voltage and capacity. Most vessels use 12 or 24 volts for their battery bank but in older vessels 110 volts is not uncommon.

Lead/acid cells consist of a series of lead plates immersed in a liquid called the electrolyte. The electrolyte in these batteries is sulphuric acid which is very corrosive, so great care must be taken when handling it.

Lead/acid batteries are popular because they are cheap and can supply high current when needed. One disadvantage is that they give off hydrogen when being charged and this is a very explosive gas. Any battery compartment must be well ventilated and care must be taken not to cause a spark near a charging battery and of course nobody working in or near the battery compartment should smoke.

As part of the chemical reaction which forms the hydrogen gas, the battery uses water which must be replaced. There are some lead/acid batteries which claim to be maintenance free, but in practice most of these eventually require that water be added. The electrolyte level should be checked at least monthly; more often if a lot of water has to be added. The recommended level of the electrolyte is usually marked inside the battery in some way. If not, then the electrolyte should be kept at such a level that the tops of the lead plates are never exposed but not so full that the electrolyte overflows when the battery is being charged. It is important to use only distilled water when topping up the electrolyte otherwise impurities will be added which will drastically shorten the life of the battery.

One big advantage of the lead/acid battery is that the relative density, or specific gravity, of the electrolyte changes according to the charge there is in the battery – the more charge that there is in the battery, the denser the electrolyte becomes. The specific gravity of the electrolyte in each cell can be easily measured using a hydrometer. This gives an accurate indication of the charge in that cell.

A hydrometer consists of a glass tube containing a float. At one end of the tube there is a rubber bulb which is used to draw a sample of the electrolyte into the tube. The float inside the tube indicates the specific gravity of the electrolyte according to how deeply or otherwise it floats in the liquid. The less dense the liquid, the deeper immersed is the float. The readings for the specific gravity of the electrolyte can be read directly off the stem of the float. The electrolyte of a fully charged lead/acid battery will have a specific gravity of about 1.26, and a fully discharged cell will give a reading around 1.16, depending on the temperature of the electrolyte.

The specific gravity reading will indicate the state of charge for each cell, so not only does it give an indication of the state of charge for the battery as a whole, but it also can give a warning of impending problems if one cell differs markedly from the others. If one cell is showing a low specific gravity, then it is an indication that that particular cell is no longer taking a full charge and it could suggest that the battery is coming to the end of its useful life.

As mentioned, great care must be taken when handling the sulphuric acid electrolyte. A sensible precaution would be to wear rubber gloves and safety goggles.

GMDSS regulations stipulate that the voltage of any secondary batteries should be read and recorded each day and in the case of lead/acid batteries, the specific gravity of the electrolyte should be measured and recorded each month.

Gel batteries

These are the modern version of the lead/acid battery. As the name suggests, the electrolyte is in the form of a gel rather than a liquid. This has the great advantage that the electrolyte cannot be spilled. Another advantage is that they do not give off hydrogen when being charged, so the possibility of an explosion is reduced and water does not need to be added.

Gel batteries can tolerate being completely discharged which lead/acid batteries cannot, and they can usually accept a charge at a higher rate than a lead/acid battery without suffering any harm.

Against all these benefits there are a couple of negatives. The first is the cost. They are at least twice the price of the equivalent lead/acid battery but generally they have a longer service life. Gel batteries do not like supplying large currents such as for starting an engine, but this is not generally a concern for batteries powering our GMDSS equipment where we are usually interested in drawing a relatively small current for a long time. The only other negative is that we cannot monitor the state of the battery with a hydrometer. The only indication we have is the voltage and this stays relatively constant until the battery is almost flat, so we may have little indication of the true state of charge of the battery. The solution is to adopt a regular pattern of charging to keep the battery well-charged.

Nickel cadmium/Nickel metal hydride batteries

Nickel cadmium batteries, or NiCads as they are usually called, face the same environmental problems of disposal as the mercury batteries. It is the cadmium which poses the problem, and they are being largely replaced by nickel metal hydride batteries. These have similar properties, but are much safer to dispose of. Both of the nickel batteries perform best if they are almost fully discharged and then fully recharged. If they are just partially discharged and then recharged on a regular basis they can lose some of their capacity. If only part of their capacity is used on a regular basis then they are said to develop a memory and their capacity will decline to more or less the amount that is regularly used.

Any of the nickel batteries will benefit from a periodic discharge to about 1 volt per cell. They should not be allowed to go below this voltage because if the battery is flattened completely, some of the cells may suffer a reversal of polarity which effectively ends the useful life of the battery. After the discharge, they should be fully recharged according to the manufacturer's recommendations.

Nickel cadmium or nickel metal hydride batteries are often found in equipment such as handheld VHFs and portable computers.

Lithium ion batteries

These are state-of-the-art rechargeable batteries. They offer at least twice the capacity of nickel metal hydride batteries and have little tendency to form a memory. The snag is that they are about three times the price of nickel metal hydride batteries. They are found in applications where a lot of power is needed but where weight or bulk must be kept to a minimum. They are often the battery of choice in top-of-the-range laptop computers.

When replacing any battery in a piece of equipment, be it primary or secondary, great care must be taken to connect it in the correct polarity. The positive (+) terminal of the battery goes to the positive (+) terminal of the equipment, which may well be coloured red. The negative (−) terminal of the battery goes to the negative (−) terminal of the equipment and this is normally coloured black. Connecting the battery the wrong way round is likely to cause serious damage.

Likewise, when charging a secondary battery the correct polarity must be observed. When connecting a portable charger, the red or positive lead from the charger must go to the positive (+) terminal of the battery. Connecting the charger the wrong way round will at best damage the battery but could even cause an explosion.

Battery Chargers

There are three main types of battery charger.

Constant voltage charger

The voltage of the charging source is set at the voltage of the fully charged battery – about 25% higher than the nominal voltage for a lead/acid battery, e.g. 15 volts for a 12 volt battery. The charging current will be high at the beginning of the charge, especially if the battery is almost flat to begin with, and then it will taper off as the battery nears capacity and its voltage rises to that of the source. The danger with this type of charger is that the initial current may be so high that the battery will get too hot, and the internal plates of the electrode could buckle and short-out.

Trickle charger

The charging current is limited to something approaching the average daily loss from the battery. The charging current might be equivalent to 1 or 2 % of the capacity of the battery. Obviously this sort of charger would be no good for recharging a battery that gets heavily discharged on a regular basis especially if the source, such as a generator, is not permanently available. A trickle charger is good for maintaining stand-by batteries in a constant state of readiness.

Constant current charger

The voltage of the source in this type of charger is perhaps 8 to 10 times higher than the voltage of the battery being charged. The current is limited by a resistor, sometimes a variable resistor, so a suitable current can be selected. The battery will be charged at a constant current with virtually no reduction even as the battery approaches full charge. The danger with this type of charger is that there can be excessive gassing or 'boiling' of the batteries in the final stages of charging. The big advantage is that the battery can be fully charged much quicker than with either of the other chargers. This type of charger is good when the battery in question is discharged regularly and the recharging source, such as a generator, is only available for limited periods. The batteries should be monitored during charging to avoid excessive gassing and fluid loss, or over heating.

Battery Maintenance

All batteries should be kept clean and dry. Any accumulation of dirt, moisture or spilled acid can allow a leakage of current between the terminals, which not only reduces the effective capacity of the battery but can also encourage corrosion. The terminals themselves should be kept clean. Lead/acid batteries often suffer a build up of white deposits on the terminals. This deposit can easily be washed off with warm water and the terminals, once they have dried, can be protected with a thin coat of petroleum jelly.

As we mentioned earlier, the GMDSS regulations for a compulsory vessel require that the batteries be tested on a regular basis – the voltage of all batteries should be measured daily and hydrometer readings taken monthly for lead/acid batteries and the results logged. For voluntary vessels it is a good idea to follow the same routine. By comparing readings of voltage and the hydrometer readings over several months an early warning of impending problems with the batteries can often be seen.

A VHF DSC transceiver. This is a stand-alone unit which does not need a DSC control unit. Note the distress button which is protected with a seal.

CHAPTER 18

Radio Log

Compulsory GMDSS vessels are required to keep a radio log in a specified format and various items must be recorded in that logbook. For non-compulsory GMDSS vessels, the various licensing authorities have differing views as to what is required but a logbook in the GMDSS format would certainly suffice.

The radio logbook itself must be kept close to the radio and it must be retained on board for inspection by any authorised person. Some administrations, such as the UK, require that the completed radio logbook for compulsory vessels be returned to them. The instructions for this are printed in the logbook.

Entries Required for Compulsory GMDSS Vessels

The GMDSS radio logbook is divided into three sections.

Section A

This contains the required particulars of the vessel such as registration information, name of owner etc., and details of the radio certification. It also states the two methods of maintenance of the equipment that have been chosen. Two of the following three methods must be chosen.

* Duplication of equipment – all essential equipment must be duplicated.
* On-board maintenance by certified engineer – this would have to be by a certified First or Second Class radio engineer.
* Shore support maintenance programme. If the shore support is chosen, details of the nominated company must be given.

Section B

This section lists the GMDSS qualified persons on board and the numbers of their certificates. Many vessels require at least two operators holding at least the General Operator's Certificate. Also in this section, the person must be named who is designated by the Master as having primary responsibility for radio communications in the event of a distress situation.

Section C

This is the diary section of the logbook. Some administrations require that this section is completed in duplicate so a copy can be retained on board when the log itself is returned to the administration. The following items must be recorded.

1. A summary of communications relating to distress, urgency or safety traffic. It must include dates, times, details of vessels involved and their positions.
2. A record of important incidents connected with the radio service, such as:
   * Any breakdown or serious malfunction of the equipment
   * Any breakdown of communications with a Coast Station, Land Earth Station or satellite
   * Adverse radio propagation conditions, such as ionospheric static, atmospheric noise or other interference
   * Serious breach of radio procedure by other stations
   * Any significant incidents concerning the exchange of commercial traffic, such as disagreement over charges or non-receipt of messages.
3. The position of the ship once a day, either in relation to a geographical point or as latitude and longitude.
4. Details and results of tests and checks carried out. These tests include:
   a. Daily:
      i. The proper functioning of the DSC equipment should be tested daily by using in-built test facilities without radiating signals.
      ii. Batteries providing energy for any part of the radio installations must be checked and if necessary brought to full charge.
      iii. Printers, including the Navtex, must be checked for an adequate supply of paper.
   b. Weekly:
      i. The proper functioning of the DSC equipment must be tested by means of a test call when within range of a DSC Coast Station. This should be done on the MF or HF calling frequencies rather than on the distress frequencies if possible. Test calls are not permitted on VHF channel 70.
      ii. Any reserve sources of power, such as a stand-by generator, must be tested weekly.
      iii. Each hand-held VHF radio for the survival craft must be tested but not on channel 16. The batteries for these radios should be charged as required.
   c. Monthly:
      i. Each EPIRB and SART should be examined monthly for signs of damage and each should be tested with its in-built test system. Care must be

taken to ensure that no signals are radiated from the EPIRB while testing.

ii. The operator must check the condition of all batteries each month and ensure that they are well secured. Terminals and connections must be checked for security and in the case of lead/acid batteries, the specific gravity of each cell should be taken and noted in the log.

iii. All antennas should be checked for condition and the antenna mounts and supports checked for security. All insulators, rigid antennas, and protective domes for satellite antennas should be cleaned as required.

In the UK, the Marine Safety Agency publish a suitable GMDSS logbook. It is available through HMSO, or any bookseller. It is called *GMDSS Radio Logbook*, and the ISBN number is 0-11-551634-4.

GMDSS approved NAVTEX receiver with built-in printer.

CHAPTER 19

Paying the Bill

Many of the services we have discussed need to be paid for. Almost without exception, arrangements for paying will have to be made in advance. Although it is possible, it would be most unwise to make credit card calls over the radio. You can rest assured that somebody, somewhere, is listening to your transmission and they could well feel tempted to 'borrow' the number of your credit card when they hear you give it to the operator and use it to make their own calls.

The charges for a call may be expressed in a number of ways. They may be priced in the national currency of the Coast Station, in US dollars, in Gold Francs or as the monetary unit of the International Monetary Fund, called the **S**pecial **D**rawing **R**ight.

The Gold Franc was based on the old French franc, but now it exists only as a unit for paying radio charges. If a Coast Station charges in Gold Francs, they will be able to give you an idea of what that means in 'real money'. The SDR is gaining popularity as a unit of charging, and 1 Gold Franc is equivalent to 3.061 SDR. The organisation with whom you contract to issue the final bill will do all the arithmetic and they will issue the bill in a currency in which you can pay.

How to Pay for Making Telephone Calls

Inmarsat

Users of Inmarsat will normally register with the company and open an account. Although calls can be made collect and by credit card, the normal way is to make calls against the account which is then settled monthly. The various services of Inmarsat are charged in different ways.

Inmarsat A and B

The two services have different rates, with B generally being cheaper. They both offer full and reduced rate calls. A direct dialled call, on voice or telex, is charged as a 6-second minimum and in 6-second increments. An operator-assisted call is charged as a 1-minute minimum and in 1-minute increments. Additional charges are levied for additional services, such as person-to-person or collect calls.

Inmarsat C,

which is data only, charges by the amount of data transmitted, rather than by time. There is a minimum charge for 256 bits of data and then in increments of 256 bits. 256 bits is 32 bytes, and for text, one byte is the same as one letter or number. Blank lines are charged as a character. Once again, there are additional charges for any additional services rendered.

Inmarsat M,

which cannot be GMDSS approved, but can support voice and data, charges a 6-second minimum and 6-second increments for self-dial calls, and a 1-minute minimum and 1-minute increments for operator-assisted calls.

MF/HF Coast Station Calls

Some Coast Stations prefer that you register with them in advance, and make arrangements for a monthly bill to paid through a bank or credit card. This would be the best system to adopt if all of your traffic regularly goes through such a Coast Station. If however you are going to use several Coast Stations then you must set up an Accounting Authority Identification Code with somebody in advance. The AAIC indicates to the Coast Station who is going to be responsible for paying the bill. AAICs are issued by registered commercial companies. British Telecom will, by prior arrangement, act as the Accounting Authority for British flag vessels. The AAIC for British Telecom is GB14. When a vessel makes a call through a Coast Station, and gives the AAIC GB14, it indicates to the Coast Station that British Telecom will pay the Coast Station and recover the money from the operator of the vessel in due course. In this computerised age most Coast Stations have instant access to a list of approved accounts for a given AAIC, which reduces the chance for fraud.

Calls are charged on a time basis – some stations having a 3-minute minimum, others 1 minute. As before, additional charges are made for any extra services.

VHF calls

Several countries offer a service where calls through Coast Stations can be charged to a shore-side telephone. This usually only works when the vessel, the Coast Station and the telephone to be charged are all of the same nationality. In the UK, this system is called YTD and was initiated primarily for yachts. For calls where such a system cannot be used, then the choices are to use an AAIC, or to make collect calls, or if you dare, credit card calls.

Some Coast Stations offer the facility for self-dial calls. These are cheaper than calls made through an operator but normally require pre-registration with the Coast Station to make billing arrangements.

The yacht on the right has an Inmarsat A dome, while the one on the left has the smaller Inmarsat M dome.

Phonetic Alphabet and Numbers

It is important to use the standardised phonetic alphabet when spelling anything over the radio, particularly if communication conditions are bad or if one or more of the operators are not native English-speakers.

International phonetic alphabet:

A	Alpha	J	Juliett	S	Sierra
B	Bravo	K	Kilo	T	Tango
C	Charlie	L	Lima	U	Uniform
D	Delta	M	Mike	V	Victor
E	Echo	N	November	W	Whiskey
F	Foxtrot	O	Oscar	X	X-ray
G	Golf	P	Papa	Y	Yankee
H	Hotel	Q	Quebec	Z	Zulu
I	India	R	Romeo		

There is a similar international system for giving numbers over the radio. It is rarely used in practice but should be learnt in case numbers such as a position have to be passed to a foreign station. When communicating with another English-speaking station then 'normal' numbers are used, but a special radio pronunciation has evolved to prevent confusion between similar sounding numbers.

	International numbers	**'Normal' radio numbers**
0	Nadazero	Zero
1	Unaone	Wun
2	Bissotwo	Two
3	Terrathree	Three
4	Kartefour	Fower
5	Pantafive	Fife

International numbers	'Normal' radio numbers
6 Soxisix	Six
7 Setteseven	Seven
8 Oktoeight	Eight
9 Novenine	Niner

Numbers over nine should always be spelled out e.g. 14 is said as Wun Fower and 29 is Two niner.

APPENDIX II

VHF Channels and Frequencies

International VHF channels, frequencies and normal use.
The use of italics indicates USA channels, frequencies and uses where different from the international allocation. All frequencies are in MHz.

Channel No.	Ship Transmit	Ship Receive	Use
01	156.050	160.650	Public Correspondence and Port Operations
01A	*156.050*	*156.050*	*Port Operations and Commercial. VTS in selected areas*
02	156.100	160.700	Public Correspondence and Port Operations
03	156.150	160.750	" " " "
04	156.200	160.800	" " " "
05	156.250	160.850	" " " "
05A	*156.250*	*156.250*	*Port Operations. VTS in Seattle*
06	156.300	156.300	Intership Safety
07	156.350	160.950	Public Correspondence and Port Operations
07A	*156.350*	*156.350*	*Commercial vessels*
08	156.400	156.400	Commercial (Intership only)
09	156.450	156.450	Intership. Commercial and Non-Commercial Secondary calling channel in many areas
10	156.500	156.500	Commercial intership and Port Operations Pollution control in UK
11	156.550	156.550	Port Operations. VTS in selected areas
12	156.600	156.600	Port Operations. VTS in selected areas
13	156.650	156.650	Intership Navigation Safety. Bridge-to-bridge
14	156.700	156.700	Port Operations. VTS in selected areas
15	156.750	156.750	Intership and Port Operations
15	*—*	*156.750*	*Environmental (Receive only). Used by Class C EPIRBs*
16	156.800	156.800	International Distress, Safety and Calling

Channel No.	Ship Transmit	Ship Receive	Use
17	156.850	156.850	Intership and Port Operations. *State Control*
18	156.900	161.500	Port Operations only
18A	*156.900*	*156.900*	*Commercial*
19	156.950	161.550	Port Operations only
19A	*156.950*	*156.950*	*Commercial*
20	157.000	161.600	Port Operations
20A	*157.000*	*157.000*	*Port Operations – simplex*
21	157.050	161.650	Port Operations
21A	*157.050*	*157.050*	*U.S. Government only*
22	157.100	161.700	Port Operations
22A	*157.100*	*157.100*	*Coast Guard Liaison and Maritime Safety Information Broadcasts*
23	157.150	161.750	Public Correspondence
23A	*157.150*	*157.150*	*U.S. Government only*
24	157.200	161.800	Public Correspondence
25	157.250	161.850	Public Correspondence
26	157.300	161.900	Public Correspondence
27	157.350	161.950	Public Correspondence
28	157.400	162.000	Public Correspondence
60	156.025	160.625	Public Correspondence
61	156.065	160.675	Public Correspondence
62	156.125	160.725	Public Correspondence
63	156.175	160.775	Public Correspondence
63A	*156.175*	*156.175*	*Port Operations and Commercial. VTS in selected areas*
64	156.225	160.825	Public Correspondence
65	156.275	160.875	Public Correspondence
65A	*156.275*	*156.275*	*Port Operations*
66	156.325	160.925	Public Correspondence and Port Operations
66A	*156.325*	*156.325*	*Port Operations*
67	156.375	156.375	UK Coast Guard primary safety channel *Commercial. Used for Bridge-to-bridge communications in lower Mississippi River. Intership only*
68	156.425	156.425	Port Operations *Non-Commercial intership*
69	156.475	156.475	Port Operations and intership *Non-Commercial intership*
70	156.525	156.525	Digital Selective Calling (voice communications not allowed)
71	156.575	156.575	Port Operations Non-Commercial
72	156.625	156.625	Non-Commercial (Intership only)
73	156.675	156.675	Port Operations. Secondary safety channel in the UK
74	156.725	156.725	Port Operations
77	156.875	156.875	Intership only. *Port Operations*

Channel No.	Ship Transmit	Ship Receive	Use
78	156.925	161.525	Public Correspondence and Port Operations
78A	*156.925*	*156.925*	*Non-Commercial vessels*
79	156.975	161.575	Port Operations only
79A	*156.975*	*156.975*	*Commercial*
80	157.025	161.625	Port Operations only
80A	*157.025*	*157.025*	*Commercial*
81	157.025	161.675	Public Correspondence and Port Operations
81A	*157.075*	*157.075*	*U.S. Government only*
			Environmental protection Operations
82	157.125	161.725	Public Correspondence and Port Operations
82A	*157.125*	*157.125*	*U.S. Government only*
83	157.175	161.775	Public Correspondence
83A	*157.175*	*157.175*	*U.S. Government only*
84	157.225	161.825	Public Correspondence
85	157.275	161.875	Public Correspondence
86	157.325	161.925	Public Correspondence
87	157.375	161.975	Public Correspondence
88	157.425	162.025	Public Correspondence
88A	*157.425*	*157.425*	*Commercial, Intership only*

NOAA Weather Radio Frequencies – Receive only:

Channel		Frequency
WX1	–	162.550
WX2	–	162.400
WX3	–	162.475
WX4	–	162.425
WX5	–	162.450
WX6	–	162.500
WX7	–	162.525

Simplex Channels for Intership HF Communications

4 MHz Band Band	6 MHz Band	8 MHz Band	12 MHz
4146 kHz	6224 kHz	8294 kHz	12,353 kHz
4149	6227	8297	12,356
	6230		12,359
			12,362
			12,365

16 MHz Band Band	18 MHz Band	22 MHz Band	25 MHz
16,528 kHz	18,825 kHz	22,159 kHz	25,100 kHz
16,531	18,828	22,162	25,103
16,534	18,831	22,165	25,106
16,537	18,834	22,168	25,109
16,540	18,837	22,171	25,112
16,543	18,840	22,174	25,115
16,546	18,843	22,177	25,118

List of Radio Signals

The Admiralty List of Radio Signals is published in six volumes, three of which are subdivided into several parts dividing the information geographically.

Volume 1. NP 281 Parts 1 and 2. **Coast Radio Stations**
Includes all frequencies and classes of emissions for Coast Stations; medical advice by radio; Inmarsat maritime satellite service; GMDSS information; piracy and armed robbery reports; regulations for use of radio in territorial waters. Part 1 covers Europe, Africa and most of Asia. Part 2 covers the Philippines, Indonesia, Australasia, the Americas, Greenland and Iceland.

Volume 2. NP 282. **Radio Navigational Aids**
Includes marine and coastal aero radio beacons; radio direction-finding stations; radar beacons such as Ramarks and Racons; time signals and legal time; electronic position fixing systems including satellite navigation systems and DGPS reference stations.

Volume 3. NP 283 Parts 1 and 2. **Radio Weather Services and Navigational Warnings**
Includes marine safety information broadcasts and some meteorological codes. Part 1 covers Europe, Africa and most of Asia. Part 2 covers Philippines, Indonesia, Australasia, the Americas, Greenland and Iceland.

Volume 4. NP284. **List of Meteorological Observation Stations**

Volume 5. NP 285. **Global Maritime Distress and Safety System**
Includes information on distress, search and rescue procedures and services available to vessels participating in the GMDSS.

Volume 6. NP 286. Parts 1, 2 and 3. **Vessel Traffic Services, Port Operations and Pilot Stations**
Includes information about pilot services and services for small craft including information on marina and harbour VHF facilities. Also includes

procedures concerning Vessel Traffic Services. Part 1 covers north-west Europe. Part 2 covers the Mediterranean, Africa and Asia. Part 3 covers Australasia, the Americas, Greenland and Iceland.

In the USA, the National Imagery and Mapping Agency (what was the Defense Mapping Agency) issue a publication number 117, called **Radio Navigation Aids.**

Chapter 1 covers Radio Direction Finding, and gives a list of RDF stations. It also lists Coast and Port Radar Stations.

Chapter 2 gives Radio Time Signal information and a list of stations broadcasting time signal information.

Chapter 3 is about Radio Navigational Warnings. It covers Coastal and Long-Range warnings broadcast by radio telephony and by Navtex.

Chapter 4 is about Distress, Emergency and Safety Traffic. It includes information about EPRIBS, Search and Rescue communications, Inmarsat and the SafetyNET system. It also covers GMDSS and DSC and lists operational DSC coast stations on VHF, MF and HF. There is also a list of frequencies monitored by the US Navy, Air Force, Coast Guard and commercial stations for HF emergency traffic.

Chapter 5 lists the stations which can handle Radio Medical Advice.

Chapter 6 is about long range navigational aids. It covers the operation of Loran-C, Omega. Decca and satellite navigation systems, both Navsat and GPS.

Chapter 7 covers AMVER – Automated Mutual-Assistance Rescue system.

Chapter 8, which we hope we will never have to refer to, covers communications in time of war and how to receive warnings of nuclear fallout.

Other good sources of radio frequency information are the Reed's Almanacs, which are published for the UK and north-west Europe, the Mediterranean and the East Coast of the USA.

Telex Service Codes and Abbreviations

Service Codes

BRK+	Breaks connection with the Coast Station
DIRTLX....+	Direct telex
FAX+	Store and forward facsimile
GA+	Go ahead, you may transmit
HELP+	List of services and codes
KKKK	Breaks connection with subscriber
MED+	Medical advice or assistance needed
MSG+	Send any traffic that you have for me
OBS+	Weather observation message
OPR+	Operator assistance requested
RTL+	Radio telex letter
TLX....+	Store and forward telex
URG+	Urgency message

Abbreviations

ABS	Subscriber not present
BK	Break
CFM	Confirm
COL	Collate
DER	Out of order
EEE	Error
INF	Contact information
MIN	Minutes
MOM	Wait

NC	No line available
OCC	Subscriber's terminal is busy
OK	Agreed
PLS	Please
PPR	Paper
QSL	Receipt acknowledged
R	Received
RAP	I will call again
RPT	Repeat
SVP	Please
TAX	What is the charge?
TEST MSG	Please send test message
THRU	You are connected, go ahead
WRU	Who are you
XXX	Error

APPENDIX VI

GMDSS Examination Syllabus

The provisions of CEPT (Conference of European Postal and Telecommunications Administrations) Recommendation T/R 31–03 require that holders of the GMDSS General Operator's Certificate have passed examinations, consisting of theoretical and practical tests in the following:

A. Knowledge of the basic features of the Maritime Mobile Service, and the Maritime Mobile Satellite Service:
    A1. The general principles and basic features of the Maritime Mobile Service.
    A2. The general principles and basic features of the Maritime Mobile Satellite Service.

B. Detailed practical knowledge and ability to use the basic equipment of a ship station:
    B1. Use in practice the basic equipment of a ship station.
    B2. Digital Selective Calling (DSC).
    B3. General principles of Narrow Band Direct Printing (NBDP) and Telex Over Radio (TOR) systems. Ability to use maritime NBDP and TOR equipment in practice.
    B4. Use of Inmarsat systems, Inmarsat equipment, or simulator in practice.
    B5. Fault locating.

C. Operational procedures and detailed practical operation of GMDSS system and
subsystems:
    C1. Global Maritime Distress and Safety System (GMDSS).
    C2. Inmarsat.

C3. NAVTEX.

C4. Emergency Position Indicating Radio Beacons (EPIRBs).

C5. Search and Rescue Transponder (SART).

C6. Distress, Urgency, and Safety communication procedures in the GMDSS.

C7. Search and Rescue operation (SAR).

D. Miscellaneous skills and operational procedures for general communications:

D1. Ability to use English language, both written and spoken, for the satisfactory exchange of communications relevant to the safety of life at sea.

D2. Obligatory procedures and practices.

D3. Practical and theoretical knowledge of general communication procedures.

Acronyms and Abbreviations

AAIC	Accounting Authority Identification Code
AC	Alternating Current
AF	Audio Frequency
AGC	Automatic Gain Control
AM	Amplitude Modulation
AMVER	Automated Mutual-assistance Vessel Rescue system
AOR	Atlantic Ocean Region
ARQ	Acknowledge Request (SITOR handshaking mode)
CEPT	Conference of European Postal and Telecommunications Administrations
CC	Command Centre (same as Operations Centre)
COSPAS	Space System for Search of Distress Vessels (a Russian Acronym)
CW	Continuous Wave (i.e. Morse code)
DC	Direct Current
DSB	Double Sideband
DSC	Digital Selective Calling
DMA	Defense Mapping Agency (US agency now called NIMA)
EGC	Enhanced Group Call (see SafetyNET)
ELT	Emergency Location Transponder
EPIRB	Emergency Position Indicating Radio Beacon
FCC	Federal Communications Commission (in USA)
FEC	Forward Error Correcting (SITOR broadcast mode)
GMDSS	Global Maritime Distress & Safety System
HF	High Frequency (3–30 MHz)
HSD	High Speed Data
HRU	Hydrostatic Release Unit
HYDROLANT	US broadcasts of Atlantic and Mediterranean Ocean navigational warnings
HYDROPAC	US broadcasts of Pacific and Indian Ocean navigational warnings
IHO	International Hydrographic Organisation
IMO	International Maritime Organisation (a UN Organisation)
Inmarsat	International Maritime Satellite Organisation
Inmarsat-A	Inmarsat mobile voice/data satellite terminal
Inmarsat-B	Inmarsat mobile voice/data satellite terminal,
Inmarsat-C	Inmarsat mobile data-only satellite terminal, also used to receive SafetyNET broadcasts
Inmarsat-E	Inmarsat EPIRB
Inmarsat-M	Inmarsat mobile voice satellite terminal (not GMDSS-compliant)
IOR	Indian Ocean Region

ITU	International Telecommunications Union (a UN Organisation)
LES	Land Earth Station – satellite equivalent to a Coast Station
LF	Low Frequency (30–300 kHz)
LUT	Local User Terminal
MAYDAY	Distress signal
MEDICO	Emergency Medical Communications
MET	Meteorological
METAREA	Meteorological Area (defined by WMO) (same as NAVAREA)
MID	Maritime Identification Digits (3-digit country identifier preceding an MMSI)
MIPDANIO	Mnemonic for sending a Mayday message
MF	Medium Frequency (0.3–3 MHz)
NIMA	National Imagery and Mapping Agency (in USA)
MMSI	Maritime Mobile Service Identity (9-digit DSC identity)
MSI	Maritime Safety Information
M/V	Motor Vessel
NAVAREA	Navigational Area (defined by IMO & IHO)
Navtex	Navigational Text (broadcast on 518 kHz)
NBDP	Narrow Band Direct Printing (ITU name for SITOR)
NCS	Network Co-ordinating Station – control station for satellites
NMEA	National Marine Electronics Association
NOAA	National Oceanic and Atmospheric Administration (in USA)
NTM	Notice to Mariners
NWS	National Weather Service (under NOAA)
OBS	Meteorological observation reports
OSC	On Scene Commander
PAN PAN	Urgency signal
PIW	Persons In the Water
POB	Persons On Board
POR	Pacific Ocean Region
RCC	Rescue Co-ordination Centre (same as OPCEN in the USA)
RF	Radio Frequency
RT	Radiotelephone
RTTY	Radioteletype – telex
SafetyNET	Considered a name, not an acronym (Inmarsat's enhanced group calling system for maritime safety broadcasts)
SAR	Search and Rescue
SART	Search and Rescue Transponder
SARNET	NOAA SARSAT Network
SARSAT	Search & Rescue Satellite-Aided Tracking
SDR	Special Drawing Rate – currency used by some Coast Stations
SECURITÉ	Safety signal (pronounced SECURITAY)
Selcall	Selective Call (sequential single frequency code)
SELFEC	Selective Forward Error Correction for telex
SHF	Super High Frequency (over 3 GHz)
SILENCE MAYDAY	Imposed silence on distress channel (pronounced 'SEELONCE MAYDAY')
SITOR	Simplex Teletype Over Radio (also radiotelex or NBDP)
SOLAS	Safety of Life at Sea Convention (treaty)
SSB	Single Sideband
STAREC	Status Recording System – new generation EPIRB
UHF	Ultra High Frequency (300 MHz – 3 GHz)
UTC	Co-ordinated Universal Time (formerly GMT)
VHF	Very High Frequency (30–300 MHz)
VLF	Very Low Frequency (3–30 kHz)
YTD	Yacht Telephone Debit. Method of paying for radio telephone calls in the UK

Index